Fun & Original
Birthday Cakes

Maisie Parrish

D&C

A DAVID & CHARLES BOOK
Copyright © David & Charles Limited 2011

David & Charles is an F+W Media Inc. company
4700 East Galbraith Road,
Cincinnati, OH 45236

First published in the UK in 2011

Text and designs copyright © Maisie Parrish 2011
Layout and photography copyright © David & Charles 2011

The author and publisher have made every effort to ensure that all
the instructions in the book are ac
cannot accept liability for any resu
persons or property, however it m

Names of manufacturers, sugarcra
are provided for the information c
to infringe copyright or trademark

A catalogue record for this book is

ISBN-13: 978-0-7153-3833-9 pape
ISBN-10: 0-7153-3833-1 paperbac

Printed in China by RR Donnelley
for David & Charles
Brunel House   Newton Abbot   Devon

Commissioning Editor: Jennifer Fox-Proverbs
Assistant Editor: Jeni Hennah
Project Editor: Ame Verso
Design Manager: Sarah Clark
Designer: Victoria Marks
Photographer: Simon Whitmore
Production Controller: Kelly Smith
Pre-Press: Jodie Culpin

David & Charles publish high quality books on a wide
range of subjects. For more great book ideas visit:
www.rucraft.co.uk

To my dear friend Fatima Robert – an
angel in disguise – and with grateful
thanks to my friends Alison and Harold

IMPORTANT NOTE
The models in this book were made using
metric measurements. Imperial conversions
have been provided, but the reader is advised
that these are approximate and therefore
significantly less precise than using the metric
measurements given. By means of example,
using metric a quantity of 1g can easily be
measured, whereas the smallest quantity given
in imperial on most modern electric scales
is ⅛oz. The author and publisher cannot
therefore be held responsible for any errors
incurred by using the imperial measurements
in this book and advise the reader to use the
metric equivalents wherever possible.

Contents

Cupcake Heaven

The Cakes

Motor Mania

The Toy Box

Retail Therapy

Golfing Dreams

The Magic Crayon

Girls' Night In

The Magic of Creating

The 'Fun & Original' series of books brings to you a superb new collection of enchanting cakes, specifically with birthdays in mind and filled with wonderful characters.

People come in all shapes and sizes with lots of different expressions, both facial and physical. Feedback from my previous books and from my workshops has told me that creating expressive characters is the key thing you wish to learn, so not only have I included more characters than ever in this book, I have also added some extra guidance in the Modelling section, to help you build your skill in crafting fun personalities.

Creating is not easy for everyone and at times can be a struggle, even for me. It is a truly magical moment when you finally arrive at that 'ah-ha!' moment. It won't happen overnight, the secret is practice, but it must always be fun. As in all my books, I have kept the instructions very simple and the beautiful photography will really help to guide you. Each character is broken down into clear steps that can be followed with ease, and you cannot fail to be thrilled with the results.

As many of you know, and some are astonished to learn, I am not a cake baker but a sugar artist who brings delicious cakes to life. My designs always have lots of details, presented in my own unique style, and this collection is no exception – it surely has something for everyone. The greatest reward about my craft is to know that my readers around the world share a love of my characters and have the same close attachment to them as I do. I know this is true because you tell me so.

Designing is a captivating process, something not everyone is capable of doing, but no matter what level you are at, once you have this book in your hands, who knows where it can take you? So jump on board and take a magical ride to your next fantastic creation!

Maisie

Sugarpaste

All the models in this book are made using sugarpaste (rolled fondant) in one form or another. This firm, sweet paste is also used to cover cakes and boards. Sugarpaste is very soft and pliable and marks very easily, but for modelling it works best if you add CMC (Tylose) to it to bulk it up (see Sugarpaste for Modelling, opposite). This section gives you the lowdown on this wonderful medium, revealing everything you need to know for success with sugarpaste.

Ready-Made Sugarpaste

You can purchase sugarpaste in the most amazing array of colours; just take it out of the packet and away you go. Of all the ready-made pastes on the market, the brand leader is Renshaws Regalice (see Suppliers, page 126), which is available in white and 14 other exciting shades. This paste is easy to work with and is of excellent firm quality.

Tip

Very dark colours, such as black, dark blue and brown, are particularly useful to buy ready-coloured, because if you add enough paste food colouring into white to obtain a strong shade, it will alter the consistency of the paste and make it much more difficult to work with.

Ready-made packaged sugarpaste is quick and convenient to use. Well-known brands are high quality and give consistently good results.

Making Your Own

While the ready-made sugarpaste is excellent, you can, of course, make your own at home. The bonus of this is that you can then tint your paste to any colour you like using edible paste food colour (see page 8). This can then be dusted with edible dust food colour to intensify or soften the shade.

Sugarpaste is such a versatile modelling medium, it can be used to create an almost endless variety of cute characters.

Sugarpaste Recipe

* 900g (2lb) sifted icing (confectioners') sugar
* 120ml (8tbsp) liquid glucose
* 15g (½oz) gelatin
* 15ml (1tbsp) glycerine
* 45ml (3tbsp) cold water

1 Sprinkle the gelatin over the cold water and allow to 'sponge'. Place over a bowl of hot water and stir with a wooden spoon until all the gelatin crystals have dissolved. Do not allow the gelatin mixture to boil.

2 Add the glycerine and glucose to the gelatin and stir until melted.

3 Add the liquid mixture to the sifted icing (confectioners') sugar and mix thoroughly until combined.

4 Dust the work surface lightly with icing (confectioners') sugar, then turn out the paste and knead to a soft consistency until smooth and free of cracks.

5 Wrap the sugarpaste completely in cling film or store in an airtight freezer bag. If the paste is too soft and sticky to handle, work in a little more icing (confectioners') sugar.

Quick Sugarpaste Recipe

* 500g (1lb 1½oz) sifted icing (confectioners') sugar
* 1 egg white
* 30ml (2tbsp) liquid glucose

1 Place the egg white and liquid glucose in a clean bowl. Add the icing (confectioners') sugar and mix together with a wooden spoon, then use your hands to bring the mixture into a ball.

2 Follow steps 4 and 5 of the above recipe for kneading and storage.

Sugarpaste for Modelling

To convert sugarpaste into modelling paste, all you need to do is add CMC (Tylose) powder (see page 25) to the basic recipe. The quantity needed will vary according to the temperature and humidity of the room, so you may need to experiment to get the right mix depending on the conditions you are working in. As a guide, add roughly 5ml (1tsp) of CMC (Tylose) to 225g (8oz) of sugarpaste and knead well. Place inside a freezer bag and allow the CMC (Tylose) to do its work for at least two hours. Knead the paste before use to warm it up with your hands; this will make it more pliable and easier to use.

If you need to make any modelled parts slightly firmer, for example if they need to support other parts, knead a little extra CMC (Tylose) into the sugarpaste.

Throughout this book I have used the combination of sugarpaste and CMC (Tylose) powder, and find it works very well. If you add too much CMC (Tylose) to the paste it will begin to crack, which is not desirable. Should this happen, knead in a little white vegetable fat (shortening) to soften the paste and make it pliable again.

Colouring Sugarpaste

Whether you choose to make your own, or to buy ready-made sugarpaste, the white variety of both forms can be coloured with paste food colours to provide a wonderful spectrum of shades.

Solid Colours

1 Roll the sugarpaste to be coloured into a smooth ball and run your palm over the top. Take a cocktail stick or toothpick and dip it into the paste food colour. Apply the colour over the surface of the sugarpaste. Do not add too much at first, as you can always add more if required.

2 Dip your finger into some cooled boiled water, shaking off any excess and run it over the top of the colour. This will allow the colour to disperse much more quickly into the sugarpaste.

3 Dust the work surface with icing (confectioners') sugar and knead the colour evenly into the sugarpaste.

4 The colour will deepen slightly as it stands. If you want to darken it even more, just add more paste food colour and knead again.

Marbled Effect

1 Apply the paste food colour to the sugarpaste as directed above, but instead of working it until the colour is evenly dispersed, knead it for a shorter time to give a marbled effect.

2 You can also marble two or more colours into a sausage shape, twist them together and then roll into a ball. Again, do not blend them together too much. Cakes and boards look particularly nice when covered with marbled paste.

Tip

When colouring white sugarpaste, do not use liquid food colour as it will make the paste too sticky.

Edible food colours come in a wide variety of forms – liquid, paste, dust and even pens – all of which can be used to add colour and life to your sugarpaste models.

Painting on Sugarpaste

There are various different ways of painting on sugarpaste. The most common way is to use paste food colour diluted with some cooled boiled water, or you can use liquid food colours and gels. There are also some food colour pens available, but these tend to work better on harder surfaces. Another way is to dilute dust food colour with clear alcohol; this is particularly useful if you want it to dry quickly. Just wash your paintbrush in clean water when you have finished.

Brushes

To paint facial features I use no.00 or no.000 sable paintbrushes. The finer and better quality the brush, the better job you will make of it. To dust the cheeks of my figures I use a cosmetics brush, which has a sponge at one end and a brush at the other. For less detailed work, you can use a variety of sable brushes in different widths.

The eyelids of this girl were dusted with Rainbow Dust sky blue edible glitter to highlight them and add interest.

Storing Sugarpaste

Sugarpaste will always store best wrapped tightly in a freezer bag, making sure you have removed as much air as possible, and then placed in an airtight container to protect it from atmospheric changes. It should be kept out of the sunlight and away from any humidity, in a cool, dry area at least half a metre (20in) off the ground. If the paste has become too dry to work with, knead in some white vegetable fat (shortening). The main thing to remember with any paste is to keep it dry, cool and sealed from the air, as this will make it dry out and go hard.

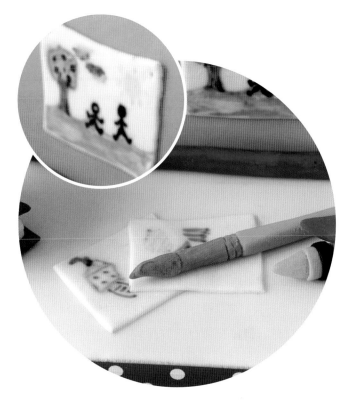

Food colour pens can be used to add quick and simple embellishments. These paintings were created with pens, as they are cleaner and easier to apply than liquid food colours.

Liquid food colour is a great way to add details such as the eyelashes on this doll, which were painted on with a no.0000 (very fine) paintbrush.

Modelling

Mastering modelling with sugarpaste is the key to creating professional-looking cakes. This section reveals all the tools and techniques you need to help sharpen your modelling skills.

General Equipment

There is a myriad of tools on the market for cake decorating and sugarcraft, but many of them are simply unnecessary. The following list gives my recommended essentials, and these are the items that form the basic tool kit listed in each of the projects in this book.

✯ **Large non-stick rolling pin**
For rolling out sugarpaste and marzipan.

✯ **Wooden spacing rods (1)**
For achieving an even thickness when rolling out sugarpaste – available in various thicknesses.

✯ **Two cake smoothers with handles (2)**
For smoothing sugarpaste when covering cakes – use two together for a professional finish.

✯ **Flower former (3)**
For placing delicate parts in while working on them so that they do not lose their shape.

✯ **Paint palette (4)**
For mixing liquid food colour or dust food colour and clear alcohol in for painting on sugarpaste.

✯ **Quality sable paintbrushes (5)**
For painting on sugarpaste and for modelling – used mainly for painting facial features and applying edible glue. The end of a paintbrush can be pushed into models to create nostrils, used to curl laces of paste around to make curly tails or hair, and used to open up flower petals.

✯ **Textured rolling pins (6)**
For creating decorative patterns in pieces of sugarpaste – for example, rice textured, daisy patterned and ribbed (see page 18).

✯ **Pastry brush (7)**
For painting apricot glaze and clear spirits onto fruit cakes.

✯ **Cutting wheel (8)**
For making smooth cuts on long pieces of sugarpaste, for use on borders mainly. A pizza cutter can be used instead.

Plastic marzipan knife
For trimming the edges of cakes and boards for a neat result.

Sugar press (9)
For extruding lengths of paste to make grass, wool, fluff and hair – a standard garlic press, found in all kitchens, is very effective for this.

Plunger cutters (10)
For cutting out different shapes in sugarpaste – such as daisies, hearts, stars and flowers.

Good-quality stainless steel cutters
Round, square, rectangle, butterfly, heart, petal/blossom – in assorted sizes. For cutting out clean shapes for use in decorations.

Frilling tool
For making frills in sugarpaste and sugar flower paste pieces – a cocktail stick or toothpick can be used instead.

Cake cards
For placing models on while working on them before transferring them to the cake.

Mini turntable (11)
Useful for placing a cake on so that it can be easily turned around while working on it – not essential.

Measuring cups (12)
For measuring out powders and liquids quickly and cleanly.

Flower stamens (13)
For creating whiskers or antennae on sugarpaste animals and insects.

Non-stick flexi mat
For placing over modelled parts to prevent them drying out – freezer bags can be used instead.

Cake boards (14)
For giving support to the finished cake – 12mm (½in) thickness is ideal.

Specific Modelling Tools

A whole book could be filled talking about these, as there are so many different varieties available. However, I use the white plastic set that has a number on each tool. I refer to the number on the tool throughout the book. They are inexpensive, light and easy to work with, and are available to buy from my website (see Suppliers, page 126).

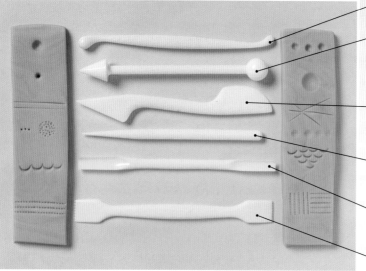

No.1 – bone tool – used to put the ears on animals.

No.3 – tapered cone/ball tool – the pointed end is used for hollowing out the bottom of sleeves and legs, making holes in the tops of bottles etc.

No.4 – knife tool – for cutting and marking fingers and toes.

No.5 – small pointed tool – used for nostrils and making holes.

No.11 – smiley tool – invaluable for marking mouths, eyelids and fish scales.

No.12 – double-ended serrated tool – for adding stitch marks on teddy bears etc.

Securing and Supporting Your Models

Sugarpaste models need to be held together in several ways. Small parts can be attached with edible glue (see page 24), but larger parts, such as heads and arms, will require additional support.

Throughout the book I use pieces of dry spaghetti for this purpose. The spaghetti is inserted into the models – into the hip, shoulder or body, for example – onto which you can attach another piece – the leg, arm or head. Leave 2cm (¾in) showing at the top to support the head, and 1cm (⅜in) to support arms and legs.

The pieces will still require some edible glue to bond them, but will have more support and will stay rigid. When inserting spaghetti to support heads, make sure that it is pushed into the body in a very vertical position otherwise the head will tilt backwards and become vulnerable.

I recommend using dry spaghetti because it is food and is much safer than using cocktail sticks or toothpicks, which could cause harm, particularly to children. However, I would always advise that the spaghetti is removed before eating the cake and decorations.

Sugarpaste models sometimes need to be supported with foam or cardboard while they are drying to prevent parts from flopping over or drooping down. Advice on where this may be necessary is given in the project instructions.

Basic Shapes

There are four basic shapes required for modelling. Every character in this book begins with a ball; this shape must be rolled first, regardless of whatever shape you are trying to make.

Ball

The first step is always to roll a ball. We do this to ensure that we have a perfectly smooth surface, with no cracks or creases.

For example:

If you pull out the ball at the front, you can shape it into an animal's face.

Sausage

From this shape we can make arms and legs. It is simple to make by applying even pressure to the ball and continuing to roll, keeping it uniform thickness along its length.

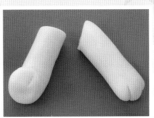

For example:

The sausage shape when turned up at the end will form a foot, or can be marked to make a paw.

Cone

This shape is the basis for all bodies. It is made by rolling and narrowing the ball at one end, leaving it fatter at the other.

For example:

The cone can be pulled out at the widest part to form the body of a bird.

Oval

This is the least used of the basic shapes, but is used to make cheeks, ears and other small parts. It is made in the same way as the sausage, by applying even pressure to the ball, but not taking it as far.

For example:

Smaller oval shapes can be used for ears.

All four basic shapes were used to make this bear – a ball for his head, a cone for his body, a sausage for his legs and an oval for his muzzle. Five of the six tools shown opposite were used in his construction.

Constructing a Head

This step-by-step demonstration shows you how to make a female head bursting with life. She has lots of details in the construction of the face.

1 Start by rolling a pear-shaped head. Add a small oval for the nose then using tool no.11, indent the top and bottom lip leaving a space in between. Join the edges at the sides (**A**).

2 Hold the head in one hand and with the little finger of your other hand, indent the eye area by rocking the shape backwards and forwards. Then, using the end of your paintbrush, push the centre of the mouth inside the head to make a cavity (**B**).

3 Roll a small banana shape for the teeth and place it under the top lip. Make two teardrop shapes in white for the eyeballs and attach just above and on either side of the nose. Add two small balls of dark blue sugarpaste to the top, and two smaller balls of black sugarpaste for the pupils. Roll two small cone shapes for the ears and attach to either side of the head, keeping the tops level with the eyes. Indent the ears at the base with the end of your paintbrush (**C**).

4 Roll two banana shapes in red sugarpaste for the lips and attach to the mouth. Outline the top and bottom of the eyes with a tiny lace of black sugarpaste and add the eyebrows in the same way (**D**).

5 Add the final details such as hair (see page 16) and earrings, highlight the eyes with a dot of white edible paint on the end of a cocktail stick or toothpick and dust the cheeks with pink dust food colour to give a healthy glow (**E**).

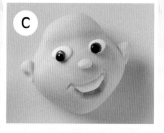
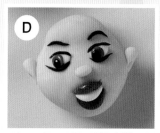
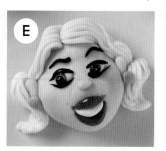

Tip
Experiment with the positioning of the eyes and eyebrows to give your characters different expressions.

A man's face has fewer details than a woman's but there are still key ways to add personality and character.

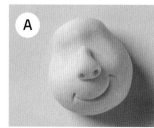
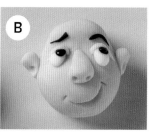
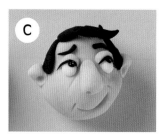

Tip
Use a flower former to hold the head in shape while you work on it.

1 After rolling the head shape and indenting the eye area (see step 2 above), add a large cone shape for the nose. Mark the nostrils with tool no.5. Press the edge of a small circle cutter below the nose to mark the mouth. Add two small lines at either end of the mouth (**A**).

2 Roll two oval shapes in white for the eyes and attach on either side of the nose. Add a small black pupil to each eye. Add small banana shapes of flesh-coloured sugarpaste for the eyelids and add the eyebrows with a thin black lace. Make two cone shapes for the ears and attach to each side, indenting them with the end of your paintbrush (**B**).

3 For the hair, roll some flattened cones of black sugarpaste and secure into style on top of the head. For the final details, add a sliver of black to outline each eyelid, highlight the eyes with a dot of white edible paint on the end of a cocktail stick or toothpick and dust the cheeks with pink dust food colour (**C**).

Using Head Shape to Add Personality

A crucial factor in imbuing your characters with personality is the shape of the head. The following examples show how using different head shapes can create a vast range of personas.

The square-shaped face implies a stocky person.

A person with a triangular face has pointed features and looks a bit shifty.

A rounded face signifies a happy personality.

This egg-shaped head would suit a studious person.

A hexagonal-shaped face indicates a bit of a thug.

The owner of this flat-shaped face would have a short, stocky body.

The pear-shaped face is the most comical and may be prone to having a double chin.

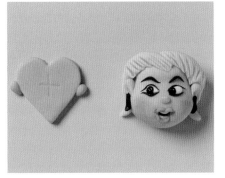

A heart-shaped face is very feminine and the hairline accentuates the shape.

An oval-shaped face is evenly balanced and is a very happy face.

Hairstyles

Hair is a great way of adding personality to your characters. For this example I will show you how to make a simple girl's hairstyle.

1 Fill the cup of a sugar press (or garlic press) with the desired colour of sugarpaste mixed with some white vegetable fat (shortening) and extrude the hair. Do not chop the hair off in a clump, but slide tool no.4 through a few strands, taking off a single layer at a time.

2 Apply edible glue around the head, and then starting at the back of the head, work around the sides adding thin layers of hair. If there is a parting at the back of the head, work from the parting to the side of the head, keeping in mind the direction in which you would comb the hair.

3 To make bunches, extrude the hair and cut off several strands together, forming a bunch. Attach to the side of the head and shape as desired.

4 For the ringlets, take three strands of hair and twist them together, make three for each side of the head. Add a ribbon to finish by rolling a small white sausage shape.

Head and Body Shapes

As you can see from the image shown below, if a body has no neck, then the neck will be modelled with the head, and likewise, if the head has a neck, then the body will be modelled without one.

Basic cone-shaped body – the head has the neck.

Shaped body with neck and shoulders – the indented head has no neck.

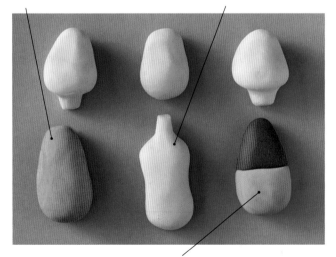

Body made in two parts by rolling two cones in different colours. Cut both cones in half and attach the top of one to the base of the other. The head for this body has a neck.

Hands and Feet

When making an arm, first roll a sausage with rounded ends. Narrow the wrist area by rolling it gently, and then narrow just above the elbow. Make a diagonal cut at the top of the arm to fit the body shape. Flatten the hand end to look like a wooden spoon.

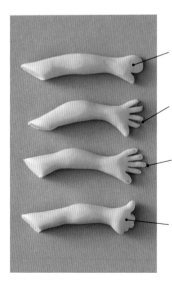

To make the hand, make a 'V' for the thumb and soften the edges with your finger.

Divide the rest of the hand into four fingers, keeping them an even width.

Roll each finger to soften the edges and mark the nails with dry spaghetti.

A less detailed hand with the fingers indented – use this when the hand does not require the fingers to be separate.

Cut out the toes as for the fingers only shorter.

Making Clothes

How you dress your characters is the final statement of their personality. Here I will show you how to make a pair of dungarees and a dress, both of which are very simple. With any clothing, you have to tailor it to the size of the body you are dressing, making sure the garments fit from side to side and from top to bottom.

Front of garment – trouser section and bib. Pockets with stitch marks add interest.

Back of garment – trouser section and braces. Patches add colour and fun.

Front of garment – square neck with a double frill and ribbon decoration.

Back of garment – high cut with a button opening. You could also add sleeves.

Shoes and Hats

Accessories such as hats and shoes are great fun to make. It is these little finishing touches that add to the charm of your finished character. Now you have lots of inspiration to create your own characters with bags of personality!

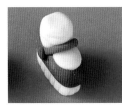

Girl's red shoe – with separate sole, strap, button detail and socks. Use dry spaghetti to attach directly to the end of the leg.

Pink slipper – with white bow. The inside is hollowed out with tool no.1 for the leg to be slipped inside.

Blue boot – with red heart tie and sole. The top is hollowed out just wide enough to fit the leg.

Black and white sports shoe – with tongue, laces and stitch marked detail. Again, the inside is hollowed out so that the leg can sit inside.

Bobble hat – formed from a cone of sugarpaste hollowed out with fingers to fit the head. Decorated with bands, stripes and furry bobbles extruded through a sugar press (or garlic press).

Cap – formed from a ball of sugarpaste, slightly flattened with a finger with a peak attached. Finished with a ball on the top and a contrasting trim around the peak.

Sun hat – made by mixing three or four different shades together to form a ball and flattening the top with a finger. A cut-out circle is attached for the brim.

Frilling

Frills can be used to decorate the side of the cake, or to make the edge of a pillow or a petticoat (see pages 92–93). You will need a special cutter called a Garrett frill cutter, which is available in two types – circle and straight. The circular cutter comes with three inner circles of different sizes to determine the depth of the frill. To make the frill, use a cocktail stick, a frilling tool, or the end of your paintbrush. Place your chosen tool on the edge of the frill and work it in a backwards and forwards motion, without putting too much pressure on it. The frill will lift where you have rolled. Continue with each section in turn until it is completed. A straight Garrett frill cutter will allow you to make a long frilled strip. The technique for frilling is exactly the same.

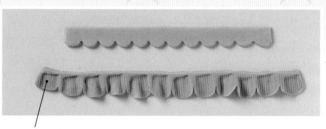

Circle cut with circle Garrett frill cutter, then frilled with a frilling tool.

A strip of continuous frill, made with a straight Garret frill cutter and frilled with the end of a paintbrush.

Texturing Sugarpaste

A great way of adding interest to your cakes is to use textured patterns in the sugarpaste. Texture can be created using impression mats or with textured rolling pins. These can be used to add designs to a large area, such as a covered cake board, or for smaller details such as clothing. Some of the fantastic textures available are shown here.

Sunflowers   Butterflies   Stars   Tulips   Roses   Fans

Bricks   Basketweave   Balloons   Lattice   Rice   Pimples

Recipes

Before you can get on with the business of decorating your cake, first you need to bake it! While there are thousands of books on cake making for you to refer to, here are my tried-and-tested recipes for both sponge and fruit cakes, for the small cakes that you will find at the end of every project, and for some additional things you will need to make.

Madeira Cake

This is a very nice firm cake that will keep for up to two weeks, giving you plenty of time to decorate it. It can also be frozen. I use it because it stays firm and will not sink when you place sugarpaste characters on the top. The recipe here is for a plain cake, but you can flavour both the sponge and the buttercream (see page 24) to suit your own taste.

Tip
The temperatures stated and baking times given are for fan-assisted ovens, which is what I use. If you are using a conventional oven, you will need to adjust the timings accordingly.

Ingredients

For a 20cm (8in) cake

★ 115g (4oz) plain flour
★ 225g (8oz) self-raising flour
★ 225g (8oz) butter (at room temperature)
★ 225g (8oz) caster sugar
★ 4 eggs

Method

1 Preheat the oven to 160°C (320°F, Gas Mark 2–3). Grease the tin and line with greaseproof paper, then grease the paper as well.

2 Sift the flours into a large mixing bowl and add the butter and sugar. Beat together until the mixture is pale and smooth. Add the eggs and beat well, adding more flour if the mixture becomes too loose.

3 Spoon the mixture into the tin, and then make a dip in the top with the back of a spoon to prevent the cake from rising too much.

4 Bake in the centre of the oven for 1–1¼ hours. Test the cake (see tip overleaf) and when it is cooked, remove it from the oven and leave it to stand in the tin for about five minutes, then turn it out onto a wire rack to cool fully.

5 Cover the cake around the sides and top with a coating of buttercream (see page 24), then cover with sugarpaste (see pages 26–27).

Rich Fruit Cake

This delicious cake improves with time, so always store it away before decorating it. I find it is generally at its best four weeks after baking, provided it is stored properly and fed with a little extra brandy!

Ingredients

For a 20cm (8in) cake

* ✭ 575g (1lb 4¼oz) currants
* ✭ 225g (8oz) sultanas
* ✭ 85g (3oz) glacé cherries
* ✭ 85g (3oz) mixed peel
* ✭ 60ml (4tbsp) brandy
* ✭ 285g (10oz) plain flour
* ✭ 2.5ml (½tsp) salt
* ✭ 1.25ml (¼tsp) nutmeg
* ✭ 3.75ml (¾tsp) mixed spice
* ✭ 285g (10oz) dark soft brown sugar
* ✭ 285g (10oz) butter (at room temperature)
* ✭ 5 eggs
* ✭ 85g (3oz) chopped almonds
* ✭ Grated zest of 1 orange and 1 lemon
* ✭ 15ml (1tbsp) black treacle

Tip

Test whether a cake is ready by inserting a fine cake skewer into the centre. If the cake is ready, the skewer will come out clean, if not, replace the cake for a few more minutes and then test it again.

Method

1 Place all the fruit and peel into a bowl and mix in the brandy. Cover the bowl with a cloth and leave to soak for 24 hours.

2 Preheat the oven to 140ºC (275ºF, Gas Mark 1). Grease the tin and line with greaseproof paper, then grease the paper as well.

3 Sieve the flour, salt and spices into a mixing bowl. In a separate bowl, cream the butter and sugar together until the mixture is light and fluffy.

4 Beat the eggs and then add a little at a time to the creamed butter and sugar, beating well after each addition. If the mixture looks as though it is going to curdle, add a little flour.

5 When all the eggs have been added, fold in the flour and spices. Then stir in the soaked fruit and peel, the chopped almonds, treacle and the grated orange and lemon zest.

6 Spoon the mixture into the prepared tin and spread it out evenly with the back of a spoon.

7 Tie some cardboard or brown paper around the outside of the tin to prevent the cake from overcooking on the outside before the inside is done, then cover the top with a double thickness of greaseproof paper with a small hole in the centre to let any steam escape.

8 Bake the cake on the lower shelf of the oven for 4¼–4¾ hours. Do not look at the cake until at least 4 hours have passed, then test it (see tip above left).

9 When cooked, remove from the oven and allow to cool in the tin. When quite cold, remove from the tin but leave the greaseproof paper on as this helps to keep the cake moist. Turn the cake upside down and wrap in more greaseproof paper, then loosely in polythene and store in an airtight tin. Store in a cool, dry place.

10 You can feed the cake with brandy during the storage time. To do this, make a few holes in the surface of the cake with a fine skewer and sprinkle a few drops of brandy on to the surface. Reseal and store as above. Do not do this too often though or you will make the cake soggy.

11 Glaze the cake with apricot glaze (see page 25), then cover with marzipan and sugarpaste (see pages 26–28).

Giant Cupcake

This is the recipe you will need in order to make the Cupcake Heaven cake on page 32, using the Wilton large cupcake pan (see Suppliers, page 126).

Ingredients

* 500g (1lb 1½oz) plain flour
* 10ml (2tsp) baking powder
* 440g (15½oz) sugar
* 440g (15½oz) soft margarine
* 7 medium eggs
* 50ml (3½tbsp) milk

Method

1 Preheat the oven to 160°C (320°F, Gas Mark 2–3).

2 Place the flour, baking powder, sugar, margarine and eggs into a mixing bowl, add the milk. Mix together with a wooden spoon and then beat for two to three minutes until smooth and glossy. Alternatively use an electric mixer and beat for one minute only.

3 Grease and flour the tin very well and fill each cavity with the cake mixture, leaving room at the top for the cake to rise. Level the top of the mixture and tap the tin to remove any air bubbles.

4 Place in the oven and cook for 1–1½ hours until the cake springs back when pressed in the centre.

5 Remove from the oven and leave the cakes in the tin to cool for 10 minutes before turning out onto a wire rack.

Mini Car Cakes

This recipe for mini cakes is used to create the small cars in the Motor Mania cake on page 40. You will need the Wilton small egg tin (see Suppliers, page 126) – this recipe will fill one tray to make eight half eggs, which will make four cars.

Ingredients

* 125g (4oz) plain flour
* 2.5ml (½tsp) baking powder
* 90g (3oz) caster sugar
* 90g (3oz) soft margarine
* 2 medium eggs
* 15ml (1tbsp) milk

Method

1 Preheat the oven to 160°C (320°F, Gas Mark 2–3).

2 Place all the ingredients into a mixing bowl and mix with a wooden spoon, then beat for two to three minutes until smooth and glossy. Alternatively use an electric mixer and beat for one minute only.

3 Grease the tin well and fill each cavity two-thirds of the way up with the cake mixture. Level the top of the mixture and tap the tin to remove any air bubbles.

4 Place in the oven and cook for 20 minutes until the cakes spring back when pressed in the centre. Remove from the oven and leave cakes in the tin to cool before turning out onto a wire rack.

5 Level the top of the cakes then sandwich two halves together with buttercream (see page 24) to form a whole egg shape.

Cupcakes

This recipe creates a wonderful vanilla-flavoured muffin-type cupcake with a rounded top, as opposed to a flatter-topped fairy cake. This recipe is used to create all the cupcakes featured in the book.

Ingredients

✱ 110g (4oz) unsalted butter (at room temperature)
✱ 130g (4½oz) sugar
✱ 3 large eggs
✱ 5ml (1tsp) pure vanilla extract
✱ 195g (7oz) plain flour
✱ 7.5ml (1½tsp) baking powder
✱ 60ml (4tbsp) milk

Method

1 Preheat the oven to 170°C (325°F, Gas Mark 3) and line 12 muffin cups with paper liners.

2 In the bowl of your electric mixer, or with a hand mixer, beat the butter and sugar until light and fluffy. Add the eggs, one at a time, beating well after each addition. Beat in the vanilla extract.

3 In a separate bowl whisk together the flour and baking powder. With the mixer on low speed, alternately add the flour mixture and milk in three additions, beginning and ending with the flour. Scrape down the sides of the bowl as needed.

4 Evenly fill the muffin cups with the mixture and bake for 18–20 minutes or until nicely browned and a skewer inserted into a cake comes out clean. Remove from oven and place on a wire rack to cool.

5 Once the cupcakes have completely cooled, frost with buttercream (see page 24) and cover with a circle of sugarpaste.

Mini Cakes

These charming mini cakes are very popular and make the main cake go much further. Children love them, especially if they are made from sponge, which you can flavour to your taste. Ideally, use the Silverwood 6cm (2½in) mini pan set (see Suppliers, page 126), but if you don't have this you can just make one large cake and cut it into individual rounds using a 5cm (2in) round cutter. Serve on 7.5cm (3in) cake cards.

Ingredients

For 16 mini cakes or one 18cm (7in) cake to be cut into rounds

✱ 250g (8¾oz) self-raising flour
✱ 250g (8¾oz) caster sugar
✱ 250g (8¾oz) butter (at room temperature)
✱ 4 eggs

Method

1 Preheat the oven to 180°C (350°F, Gas Mark 4), and prepare the cake pans with silicone liners or with greaseproof paper.

2 Prepare the mixture as for the Madeira cake (see page 19) and half fill each cake pan. Bake in the centre of the oven for 15–20 minutes. You may wish to put a baking sheet on the bottom shelf to catch any drips. When cooked, remove from the oven and allow to cool to room temperature.

3 Leave the cooled cakes in the pans and slice neatly across the tops with a long-bladed knife, using the pan tops as a cutting guide.

4 Remove the pans from the base and gently pull the halves apart to remove the cakes. You may need to run a thin-bladed knife around the top edges to release any slight overspill. Place the cakes on a wire rack. Once cooled, keep them covered, as they will dry out very quickly.

5 Cover each cake around the sides and top with a coating of buttercream (see page 24), then cover with rolled sugarpaste (see pages 26–27).

Sugar Flower Paste

This is a good strong paste that can be rolled very thinly. It is ideal for making delicate objects such as flowers and butterflies. It is used to make the windscreen (windshield) on the car in the Motor Mania cake on page 40.

Ingredients

★ 3 medium egg whites (at room temperature)
★ 594g (1lb 5oz) icing (confectioners') sugar
★ 20g (¾oz) CMC (Tylose) powder (see page 25)
★ 14g (½oz) white vegetable fat (shortening)

Method

1 Lightly beat the egg whites in a mixing bowl. Sieve the icing (confectioners') sugar and gradually add it to the egg whites beating well between additions until a soft peak consistency is reached.

2 Add the CMC (Tylose) powder and white vegetable fat (shortening). Beat again – it will thicken immediately.

3 Remove from the bowl and knead well for a few minutes until soft, smooth and stretchy.

4 Put into strong polythene bag immediately then into an airtight container. The paste will keep for many weeks and can be stored in the fridge.

Pastillage

Pastillage is a form of sugarpaste that dries very hard so is ideal for pieces that need to remain rigid such as the toy box on page 52 and the headboard on page 114.

Ingredients

★ 2 medium egg whites
★ Dust food colour in the desired shade
★ 14oz (½oz) icing (confectioners') sugar
★ 10ml (2tsp) CMC (Tylose) powder (see page 25)

Method

1 Place the egg whites into a mixing bowl and beat.

2 Add the dust food colour to the sifted icing (confectioners') sugar, and add gradually to the egg whites, beating after each addition.

3 When all the sugar has been added, mix in the CMC (Tylose) powder to form a stiff paste.

4 Remove the mixture from the bowl and knead into a smooth paste. Wrap tightly in a freezer bag and place in the fridge until required.

Tip

You will need to repeat this recipe five times to complete The Toy Box cake on page 52. It is best to make one mix at a time so as not to overload your mixer.

Edible Glue

This is the glue that holds sugarpaste pieces together, used in every project in this book. Always make sure your glue is edible before applying it to your cake.

Ingredients

★ 1.25ml (¼tsp) CMC (Tylose) powder
★ 30ml (2tbsp) boiled water, still warm
★ A few drops of white vinegar

Method

1 Mix the CMC (Tylose) powder with the warm boiled water and leave it to stand until the powder has fully dissolved. The glue should be smooth and to a dropping consistency. If the glue thickens after a few days, add a few more drops of warm water.

2 To prevent contamination or mould, add a few drops of white vinegar.

3 Store the glue in an airtight container in the fridge and use within one week.

Tip
To make a stronger edible glue, add an extra pinch of CMC (Tylose) to the basic recipe and mix into a stiff paste.

Buttercream

A generous coating of buttercream precedes the covering of sugarpaste on all sponge cakes. The classic version is flavoured with a few drops of vanilla essence, but you could substitute this for cocoa powder or grated lemon/orange zest to suit your particular taste.

Sweet and delicious, buttercream is simple to make and is the ideal covering for both large and mini sponge cakes. Smooth on a generous layer with a palette knife before they are covered in sugarpaste.

Ingredients

To make 480g (1lb) of buttercream

★ 110g (4oz) butter (at room temperature)
★ 30ml (2tbsp) milk
★ 350g (12oz) sifted icing (confectioners') sugar

Method

1 Place the butter into a mixing bowl and add the milk and any flavouring required.

2 Sift the icing (confectioners') sugar into the bowl a little at a time. Beat after each addition until all the sugar has been incorporated. The buttercream should be light and creamy in texture.

3 Store in an airtight container for no more than one week.

CMC (Tylose) powder, white vegetable fat (shortening), apricot glaze and confectioners' glaze are essential products that you will need to purchase before you begin sugarcrafting (see Suppliers, page 126).

Essential Purchases

A visit to your local cake decorating or sugarcraft shop is a must – not only can you buy all the necessary products there, you will also come away very inspired! These products cannot be made at home with any great ease, and therefore need to be purchased.

☆ White vegetable fat (shortening)

This is used for softening sugarpaste so that it can be extruded through a sugar press more easily to make hair, grass, fluff etc. If you find your sugarpaste has dried out a bit, knead in a little of this to make it soft and pliable again.

☆ CMC (Tylose) powder

Carboxymethylcellulose is a synthetic and inexpensive thickening agent that is used to convert sugarpaste into modelling paste (see page 7), and also used for edible glue.

☆ Apricot glaze

This glaze is painted onto fruit cakes before adding a layer of marzipan (see page 28). It is made from apricot jam, water and lemon juice, which is boiled then sieved. Although it would be possible to make your own, I don't know anyone who does, as it is so easy to use straight from the jar.

☆ Confectioners' glaze

This product is used to highlight the eyes, shoes, or anything you want to shine on your models. It is particularly useful if you want to photograph your cake, as it will really add sparkle. Apply a thin coat and let it dry, then apply a second and even a third to give a really deep shine. It is best kept in a small bottle with brush on the lid – this way the brush is submerged in the glaze and doesn't go hard. If you use your paintbrush to apply it, then you will have to clean it with special glaze cleaner.

Covering Cakes

Most beginners can successfully cover a cake with sugarpaste. However, a professional finish – a glossy surface free of cracks and air bubbles with smooth rounded corners – will only result from practice.

1 Prepare the cake with a layer of buttercream (see page 24) or apricot glaze and marzipan (see page 28) depending on whether it is a sponge or a fruit cake.

2 Take sufficient sugarpaste to cover the complete cake. The quantity required for each of the cakes in this book is given at the start of each project. Work the paste until it is quite soft and smooth, then place it onto a surface lightly dusted with icing (confectioners') sugar.

3 Roll out the paste with a non-stick rolling pin – spacing rods can be used to maintain a uniform thickness (**A**). The depth of the paste should be approximately 5mm (⅛in). As you roll the paste, move it regularly to ensure it has not stuck to the surface.

4 Measure the cake by taking a measuring tape up one side, over the top and down the other side. The sugarpaste should be rolled out in the shape of the cake to be covered (round for a round cake, square for a square cake and so on), and rolled out a little larger than the measurement just made.

Tip

When covering a cake, try to do it in natural daylight, as artificial light makes it more difficult to see flaws. Sometimes imperfections can be covered, but sometimes they will occur where you are not going to put decorations so you need to strive for a perfect finish every time. However, if things don't go to plan, don't worry; the sugarpaste can be removed and re-applied.

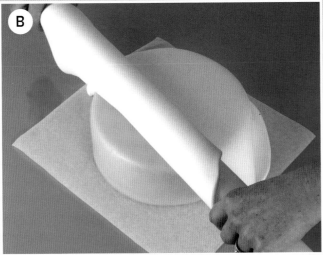

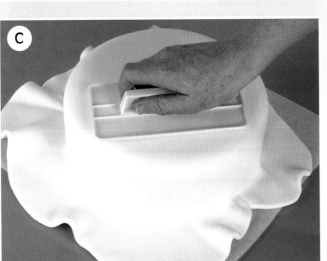

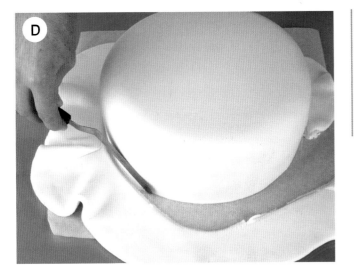

5 Lift and drape the paste over the cake using a rolling pin (**B**). Carefully lift the sides of the paste, brushing the top surface of the cake in one direction to eliminate any air trapped in between. Continue to smooth the top with the palm of your hand and then use a smoother (**C**).

6 For the sides, lift, flatten and rearrange any folds at the bottom removing any creases. Do not smooth downwards as this may cause a tear at the top edge. With your hand, ease the sugarpaste inwards at the base and smooth the sides with an inward motion using your hand and a smoother.

7 Trim the bottom edge with a marzipan knife (**D**). Trim the paste in stages as the icing shrinks back.

8 Check the surface and sides for any flaws and re-smooth if necessary. For air bubbles, insert a pin or fine needle into the bubble at an angle and gently rub the air out, then re-smooth to remove the tiny hole.

9 Once you are happy with the surface, use either the smoother or the palm of your hand and polish the top of the cake to create a glossy finish.

10 Ideally the sugarpaste should be left to dry for one or two days at room temperature before the cake is decorated.

Tip

Keep the dusting of icing (confectioners') sugar on the work surface very light; too much will dry out the paste and make it crack.

Covering the Cake Board

Moisten the board with cooled boiled water, then roll out the specified quantity of sugarpaste to an even thickness, ideally using spacing rods (see page 26). Cover the board completely with sugarpaste using the same method as for the covering of the cake, smoothing the paste out and trimming the edges neatly with a marzipan knife. Some paste can then be saved by removing a circle from the centre of the board, which will be covered by the cake. For a professional finish edge the board with ribbon, securing it with non-toxic glue.

Tip

An alternative method for covering a board involves placing the cake on to the board prior to covering them, then using a single piece of sugarpaste to cover them both. The sugarpaste needs to be rolled out much larger for this method.

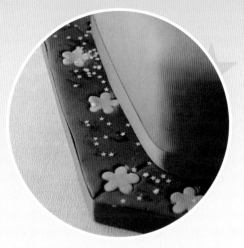

Covering the cake board in sugarpaste gives your cakes a really professional appearance and allows you to add extra decorations and embellishments. As a finishing touch, edge the board with a length of toning ribbon.

Covering a Cake with Marzipan

A layer of marzipan is used on fruit cakes only. Sponge cakes should be covered with buttercream (see page 24) prior to covering with sugarpaste. For fruit cakes, coat first with apricot glaze (see page 25) as this will help the marzipan to stick. The quantity of marzipan required will depend on the size of the cake, but as a general guide, half the weight of the cake will give you the correct weight of marzipan.

1 Place the glazed cake onto a sheet of greaseproof paper. Place the marzipan in between spacing rods and roll to an even thickness large enough to cover the cake.

2 Lift the marzipan onto the rolling pin and place it over the cake. Push the marzipan into the sides of the cake using a cupped hand to ensure there are no air pockets.

3 Trim off any excess marzipan with a knife and then run cake smoothers along the sides and the top of the cake until they are straight.

4 Leave the marzipan to dry for one or two days in a cool temperature.

5 Before applying the sugarpaste, sterilize the surface of the cake by brushing the marzipan with a clear spirit such as gin, vodka or kirsch. Ensure the entire surface is moist; if there are any dry areas the paste will not stick to the marzipan and could result in air bubbles.

Tip

If you are using marzipan, make sure nobody eating the cake is allergic to nuts. This is very important as nut allergies are serious and can have fatal consequences.

Dowelling Cakes

A stacked cake is dowelled to avoid the possibility of the upper tiers sinking into the lower tiers. The Retail Therapy cake (page 70) is the only cake that requires dowelling but you could use this technique to add extra tiers to any of the other cakes, if you want to adapt the designs.

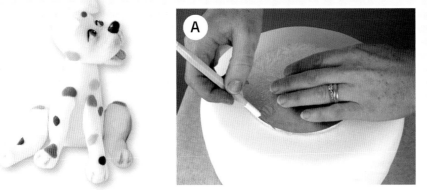

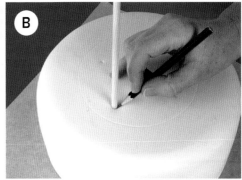

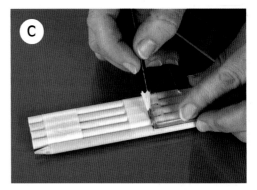

1 Place a cake board the same size as the tier above in the centre of the bottom tier cake. Scribe around the edge of the board (**A**) leaving an outline and then remove the board.

2 Insert a wooden dowel vertically into the cake 2.5cm (1in) from the outline, down to the cake board below. Take a pencil and mark the dowel level with the surface of the cake (**B**) and then remove the dowel.

3 Tape together the number of dowels required (four is usually sufficient), and then draw a line across using the marked dowel as a guide (**C**). You can then saw across all the dowels to make them exactly the same length. Alternatively, you can unwrap the marked dowels and cut each of them separately with a pair of pliers or strong kitchen scissors.

4 Place the cut dowel back into the hole, then arrange the other dowels into the three, six and nine o'clock positions to the first one (**D**). Ensure that all the inserted dowels are level and have flat tops.

5 The cake board of the upper tier should rest on the dowels and not on the cake. The very slight gap in between the cake and the board of the upper tier will not be noticed and is normally covered by decoration.

Have Your Cake and Eat It!

You may well have cooked up a storm and made the perfect party cake, but how do you get your creation from kitchen to guest without a hitch? Storing the cake ahead of the event is the first consideration, then, if the party is not at your home, transporting it to the venue in one piece is of primary importance. Finally, some top tips follow on cutting the cake and removing items before eating it.

Cake Boxes

The most essential item for safe storage and transportation of your cake is a strong box designed for the job. You can buy special boxes for stacked cakes (see Suppliers, page 126) that open up at the front to enable the cake to slide inside. The front then closes and finally the lid is placed on the top. Make sure the box is deep and high enough to take the cake without damaging it when the lid goes on. To make the cake even safer inside the box, you can buy non-slip matting from most DIY stores. A piece of this cut to size and placed under the cake board will prevent it moving around inside the box.

Tip
Keep your cakes away from direct sunlight at all times, as bright light will fade the sugarpaste.

Room Temperature

The temperature of the room the cake is stored in is crucial to its condition. If your house or the party venue is very humid it can be disastrous. You would do well to invest in a portable dehumidifier to keep the moisture at bay, especially during wet weather. Never think that your figures will benefit from leaving a heater on in the room; you will find that they become too warm and soft and will flop over.

Transportation

If you are transporting a cake, you need to be sure that the boot (trunk) of the car is high enough when closed, and the cake itself is made secure on a flat surface for the journey. Never put the cake on the back seat of the car, as this is not a level surface and the cake could be ruined when you apply the brakes. Remember too that if the vehicle gets too hot, it will affect the cake. It can melt buttercream and make sugarpaste soft.

Cutting the Cake

Many people have no idea how to begin to cut a cake, particularly a stacked one. If it is not cut properly it could end up in a pile of crumbs. The number of portions you require will have some bearing on the way you cut the cake. A simple way is to mark points on the edge of the cake at the desired intervals. Use a sharp serrated knife to cut across the cake and then downwards keeping the blade of the knife clean at all times. Then cut the section into smaller pieces.

The Decorations

If you wish to keep the decorations or figures on the cake, remove them before cutting. If they are to be stored, then do not put them into a plastic container, as they will sweat. Place them inside a clean cardboard box wrapped in tissue paper. Your decorations and figures will keep for a long time if you make sure they are kept in a dry atmosphere. Should you wish to display them, the best place is inside a glass-fronted cabinet where they will be safe.

Any decorations with wires attached should never be inserted directly into the cake as the metal can cause contamination. Instead, insert a cake pick, pushing it right into the cake until the top is level with the surface, then place the wires inside. Alternatively, you can make a mound of sugarpaste to insert wires into, and this can be hidden with more decoration.

When making figures for your cake, never insert cocktail sticks, always use pieces of dry raw spaghetti. Remove these before eating the figures. Children will always want to eat the figures, no matter how long it has taken you to make them.

Tip

If you wish to add candles to decorate your cake, always insert the candle holder into the cake first. When the candles are lit, they will prevent any wax from spilling on to the cake. Remove them before cutting the cake.

Frequently Asked Questions

Q: What if the road I am taking to deliver the cake is very bumpy?
A: Place the cake on a flat surface in the car. If necessary place a foam mat under the box and drive slowly!

Q: Is the foot well of the car the best place to transport a cake?
A: It is a good place, but make sure that there is nothing on the seat to slide off on to the cake – with disastrous consequences.

Q: What if it is a really hot day when the cake is delivered?
A: Keep the air conditioning on if you have it.

Q: If the cake is too heavy for me to lift at my destination what should I do?
A: Never try to lift a large cake on your own; ask if there is a truck available, or even a small table on wheels to place it on.

Q: Where is the cake best displayed?
A: Try to display the cake in a tidy, uncluttered area that will not detract from the design.

Q: What should I look for once the cake has been assembled?
A: Check that the ribbon around the board is still lined up correctly and has not become loose or dislodged. Make sure your cake topper is securely fixed and perfectly upright.

Q: What shall I do if I make a mark on the cake while I am transporting it to its destination?
A: Always carry a fixing kit with you, which should include edible glue, a little royal icing in a bag, and a few spare decorations you can apply to cover the mark, depending on the design of the cake.

Cupcake Heaven

This giant cupcake is a real showstopper but is the perfect cake for beginners as it uses simple techniques and easy-to-make decorations. The shape may look complicated but it is made using a special tin. This cake is such fun to make and can be decorated in so many different ways to suit just about everyone!

"It will be smiley faces all round when they see this cake!"

You will need

Sugarpaste

* 721g (1lb 9½oz) orange
* 235g (8¼oz) yellow
* 224g (8oz) pink
* 30g (1oz) red
* 1g (⅛oz) black

Materials

* Giant cupcake (see recipe, page 21)
* Buttercream (see page 24)
* Fuchsia liquid food colour
* Rainbow Dust sparkle stars
* Silver sugar dragees
* Edible glue (see page 24)

Equipment

* Wilton large cupcake pan
* 13cm (5in) cake card
* 3cm (1¼in), 2.5cm (1in) and 1.5cm (½in) round cutters
* 3.5cm (1⅜in) butterfly cutter
* 3.5cm (1⅜in) star cutter
* 4cm (1½in) and 2cm (¾in) blossom cutters
* Basic tool kit (see pages 10–12)

Covering the base cake . . . .

1 Make the giant cupcake using the Wilton large cupcake pan and the recipe on page 21 (**A**). Once the cakes have cooled, put them into the freezer, as this will allow you to carve them without crumbling. Place the base cake onto a 13cm (5in) cake card, and then onto a sheet of greaseproof paper. Using a very sharp knife, slice off the top to make it level. Take the top cake and slice that level, and then set it aside.

A

2 Coat the side and top of the base cake with a thin layer of buttercream and then apply to the top cake.

Tip
When applying the buttercream and sugarpaste to the side of the cake, use your fingers to get into the grooves to keep the shape defined.

3 To cover the base cake roll out 250g (8¾oz) of orange sugarpaste to a measurement of 10 x 50cm (4 x 20in). As you roll out the paste do so in a curve, just like the shape of a cupcake wrapper (**B**). Do not make the sugarpaste any thicker than 5mm (⅛in) as if you do you will hide the lines on the side of the cake. Make a perfect join at the back so that the paste does not overlap (see tip, below right).

4 Define the shape by gently running a clean finger inside the grooves. Trim around the base neatly, as the cake card should not show. Allow the paste to overlap on the top to about 1.5cm (½in).

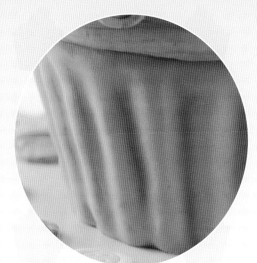

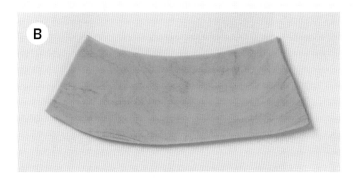
B

Tip

To make a perfect join, overlap the edges and cut through both layers. Remove the excess to leave two straight edges that fit together neatly.

Covering the top cake . . . .

1 To cover the top cake roll out a further 250g (8¾oz) of orange sugarpaste. Using your finger, gently smooth the sugarpaste into the grooves then trim the base of the cake neatly, leaving 1cm (⅜in) of extra sugarpaste around the edge. Place the cake on top of the base cake, turning the extra paste under to give a rounded finish. You should be able to see the lovely swirl all around the top of the cake.

2 To make the swirls for the top of the cake you will need 200g (7oz) each of yellow, pink and orange sugarpaste. Make the pink sugarpaste look striped by adding a few drops of fuchsia liquid food colour and kneading it into the paste, being careful not to over mix it. Add together 100g (3½oz) of the yellow, orange and pink striped sugarpaste and marble to make a sausage shape (see page 8). Place the sausage onto the work surface and using your rolling pin, thin the bottom half of the sausage leaving the top half thick (**C**).

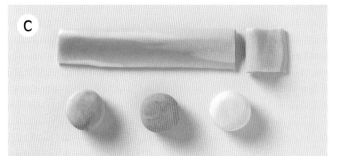
C

3 Apply some edible glue to the top of the cake and begin to wind the strip around from the top to the bottom. You will have to join it at the back and continue with another strip using the remainder of the sugarpaste until the whole top of the cake is covered.

Tip
When creating the swirl, wind the sausage shape round with the thickest part at the top.

The giant decorations

1 To make the flowers you will need 5g (¼oz) each of yellow, pink and orange sugarpaste. Using a 4cm (1½in) blossom cutter, cut out a shape in each colour then using a 2cm (¾in) blossom cutter, cut out a smaller shape in each colour. Mix up the colours and attach a small flower to the centre of a large flower, and add a small round ball of the final colour in the centre. Add a small silver dragee in the centre of each. Make three assorted coloured flowers and set aside to dry (**D**).

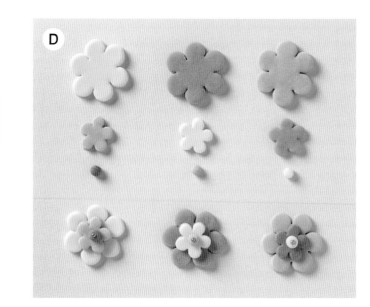

2 To make the hearts equally divide 30g (1oz) of red sugarpaste into three and roll into balls then into soft cone shapes. Using tool no.4, mark a division in the top of each cone then soften the edges with your fingers. Taper the end of each heart and set aside to dry (**E**).

3 For the three butterflies you will need 3g (⅛oz) each of pink, yellow and orange sugarpaste randomly mixed together and rolled out. Cut out three shapes with the butterfly cutter and set aside to dry (**E**).

4 For the stars roll out 3g (⅛oz) of pink sugarpaste and cut out three shapes using the star cutter, then set aside to dry (**E**).

Tip
To give the butterflies more shape, leave them to dry in a former, made from a piece of bent cardboard.

5 **For the buttons** roll out 6g (¼oz) each of pink, yellow and orange sugarpaste. Cut out one 3cm (1¼in) circle and one 2.5cm (1in) circle in each colour to make a large and small button. Indent the large button with the 2.5cm (1in) round cutter and indent the small button with the 1.5cm (½in) round cutter. Using tool no.5, mark four holes in the centre of each button and set aside (**F**).

Tip
You can make some extra buttons in the same way to decorate the plate or cake stand as desired.

6 **Make the Catherine Wheel** by randomly mixing together 4g (⅛oz) each of the pink, yellow and orange sugarpaste. Roll into a sausage shape and curl it around to make the wheel. Secure with edible glue and set aside to dry (**F**). Make a smaller wheel using 3g (⅛oz) of each colour randomly mixed together and place a silver sugar dragee in the centre.

7 **To make the smiley faces** you will need 14g (½oz) of yellow sugarpaste and 1g (⅛oz) of black. Roll out and cut three circles using a 2.5cm (1in) round cutter. Add two small balls of black sugarpaste for the eyes then roll a very small lace in black to make the smile and the hair. For the moustache, just turn up the end of the lace to shape (**F**).

8 **To complete the cake** arrange the decorations around the cake, securing with edible glue. Push a piece of dry spaghetti into the top of the cake and slip the large Catherine Wheel over the top. Add some Rainbow Dust sparkle stars to finish.

A Little More Fun!

Mesmerizing Muffins

The motifs from the main cake can be used on matching standard-sized cupcakes too (see recipe, page 22). With small cakes it is better to simplify things, so just choose one design and place it on top of a large sugarpaste swirl. Try marbling different quantities of the colours together for the swirls so that each cake is unique yet they all coordinate. Paper cases complete the look and are an easy way to create a professional finish.

Motor Mania

There are some things a man puts first in his life, and his car and his dog are usually high on his agenda! This is the perfect cake for any motoring fan and can easily be adapted to depict a younger driver or a different breed of dog. Use the space on the number (license) plate to write his name and age or his cherished personalized registration.

"Move over Rover, we've got some serious driving to do!"

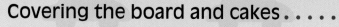

You will need

Sugarpaste

* 1kg 550g (3lb 6½oz) green
* 640g (1lb 6½oz) yellow
* 260g (9oz) black
* 232g (8⅛oz) white
* 79g (2¾oz) red
* 65g (2¼oz) blue
* 59g (2oz) orange
* 48g (1⅝oz) dark green
* 45g (1½oz) light brown
* 28g (1oz) flesh
* 28g (1oz) dark brown
* 2g (⅛oz) pink

Materials

* 25cm (10in) round cake
* 25 x 18cm (10 x 7in) cake
* 8 half egg mini cakes (see recipe, page 21)
* Buttercream (see page 24)
* 5g (¼oz) sugar flower paste (see page 23)
* Dust food colour in silver metallic and pearl lustre
* Black food colour pen
* White vegetable fat (shortening)
* Edible glue (see page 24)
* Non-toxic glue

Equipment

* 40cm (16in) round cake drum
* 23cm (9in) cake cards
* Silverwood 30 x 10cm (12 x 4in) multi-size cake pan
* Wilton mini egg pan (see Suppliers, page 126)
* 6cm (2⅜in), 3cm (1¼in), 2.5cm (1in), 2cm (¾in), 1.5cm (½in) and 1cm (⅜in) round cutters
* 2.5cm (1in) square cutter
* Green ribbon 15mm (½in) wide x 1.5m (59in) long
* Basic tool kit (see pages 10–12)

Covering the board and cakes . . . .

1 To cover the board roll out 1kg (2lb 3¼oz) of green sugarpaste to an even 3mm (⅛in) thickness. Cover the board in the usual way (see page 28) then trim the edges neatly. Place a 23cm (9in) cake card in the centre of the covered board and mark around the edges. Lift out the circle of sugarpaste and this will save you 450g (1lb). Set the board aside to dry.

2 To cover the cake add the leftover 450g (1lb) of green sugarpaste to a further 550g (1lb 3¼oz) making 1kg (2lb 3¼oz). Roll out to a 5mm (⅛in) thickness and cover the cake in the usual way (see pages 26–27). Attach the cake to the board with strong edible glue (see page 24), positioning the cake two finger-widths from the edge of the board. Edge the board with the green ribbon, securing it with non-toxic glue.

3 To complete the chequered border you will need 100g (3½oz) of black sugarpaste and 100g (3½oz) of white. Roll out to an even 3mm (⅛in) thickness. Cut out the squares using a 2.5cm (1in) cutter. Begin on the bottom row by cutting the squares in half, gluing them all around the base of the cake. Add the middle row with the opposite colour on the top, and finally the top row with the squares cut in half again (**A**).

A

The large car

1 For the car take the 25 x 18cm (10 x 7in) cake and freeze it to prevent it crumbling during shaping. Cut the cake in half and sandwich the two layers together with buttercream or your favourite filling, then carve the cake into a smooth egg shape. Using a 6cm (2⅜in) round cutter, take out the seat area (**B**), then prepare the cake as desired (see page 26). Roll out 500g (1lb 1½oz) of yellow sugarpaste to a 5mm (⅛in) thickness. Gently press it into the seat area and arrange over the sides and underneath to completely cover it. Place the car onto a cake card dusted with icing (confectioners') sugar.

2 Make up 145g (5⅛oz) of grey sugarpaste by mixing 125g (4½oz) of white with 20g (¾oz) of black. For the radiator grill, roll out 16g (½oz) of the grey sugarpaste. Cut out a rectangle measuring 8 x 2.5cm (3⅛ x 1in) and angle it at either end. Mark the lines across the grill using the edge of a ruler (**C**). Dust with a dry brush and silver metallic dust food colour. Attach to the front of the car with edible glue. Roll the leftover paste into a thin lace and attach around the top and sides of the grill.

3 For the boot (trunk) take 12g (½oz) of yellow sugarpaste, roll out and cut out a 6cm (2⅜in) circle, then make a straight edge by taking off 1cm (⅜in). Attach to the centre back of the car. Roll a small sausage shape of grey for the handle and mark with tool no.4 (**C**).

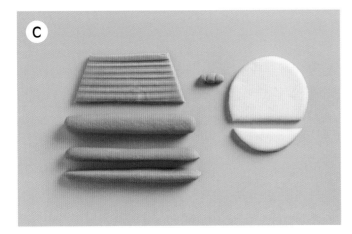

4 For the bumpers you will need 12g (½oz) of grey sugarpaste rolled into a sausage shape 9cm (3½in) long. Cut in half lengthwise (**C**), apply some edible glue and attach one half underneath the radiator grill. Attach the other half to the back of the car under the boot (trunk). Dust the bumpers and the boot (trunk) handle with pearl lustre dust food colour.

5 For the number (license) plate you will need 4g (⅛oz) of white sugarpaste rolled out thinly. Cut a strip measuring 1.5 x 5cm (½ x 2in) and attach to the bonnet (hood) of the car in an arched shape (**D**). Use a black food colour pen to write your desired text on the plate.

6 Make the headlights using 6g (¼oz) of black sugarpaste equally divided. Roll into two balls and flatten with your finger. Using a 1.5cm (½in) round cutter and 2g (⅛oz) of grey sugarpaste rolled out thinly, cut two circles and place one in the centre of each headlight (**D**). Push a short piece of dry spaghetti into the radiator grill and attach the lights securely.

7 For the wheels divide 80g (2⅞oz) of black sugarpaste equally into four and roll into balls then flatten with your fingers. Roll out 10g (⅜oz) of grey sugarpaste and cut out four 2cm (¾in) circles. Mark lines from the centre as shown using tool no.4. Attach to the centre of each wheel and finish with a small flattened ball in the centre (**D**). Allow the wheels to dry before attaching them to the car.

8 For the headrests roll out 15g (½oz) of grey sugarpaste to a 3mm (⅛in) thickness. Cut out two 3cm (1¼in) circles and made a straight edge on each (**E**). Attach to the back of the seat area.

9 Make a roll to go around the top of the car using 7g (¼oz) of grey sugarpaste. Attach with edible glue finishing at the back of the headrests.

10 For the folded-down convertible top roll out 40g (1½oz) of grey sugarpaste into a rectangle measuring 9 x 8cm (3½ x 3⅛in). Fold it without creasing it (**E**) and attach behind the headrests.

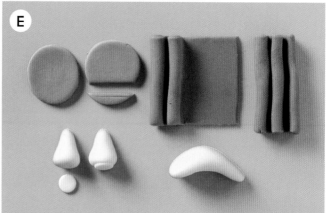

11 **To make the wing (side) mirrors** equally divide 6g (¼oz) of yellow sugarpaste and roll into two cone shapes. Flatten the end of each cone with your finger and attach a small circle of white sugarpaste cut using a 1.5cm (½in) round cutter (**E**). Attach one to each side of the car. Insert a short piece of dry spaghetti into the body of the car, attach the wheels and secure with edible glue.

12 **Make the wheel arches (fenders)** by dividing 64g (2¼oz) of yellow sugarpaste equally into four. Roll each portion into a soft cone shape and flatten with your finger, keeping it nicely rounded (**E**). Apply edible glue over the top of the wheels and attach to the car.

13 **Make the side (parking) lights** for the front and back using 10g (⅜oz) of grey sugarpaste. Cut out two 2cm (¾in) and two 1.5cm (½in) circles and dust with silver metallic dust food colour. Add a 1cm (⅜in) circle of grey sugarpaste to the centre of each light and dust with pearl lustre dust food colour (**F**).

14 **To make the windscreen (windshield)** mix 5g (¼oz) of sugar flower paste with a tiny pinch of black sugarpaste to make an even grey shade. Cut a strip measuring 11cm x 4mm (4½ x ⅛in), curve each end downwards to shape (**F**) and place on a flat surface to dry, turning it over once during drying.

15 **For the steering wheel** roll out 5g (¼oz) of grey sugarpaste and cut out a 2.5cm (1in) circle. Take out the centre using a 2cm (¾in) round cutter (**F**). Place on a flat surface to dry.

16 **For the dashboard** you will need 15g (½oz) of dark brown sugarpaste. Roll into a thick sausage shape and flatten slightly (**F**). Attach to the front of the car and secure the steering wheel into position on the right of the car (see tip, right). The windscreen (windshield) will be attached once the figures are in place.

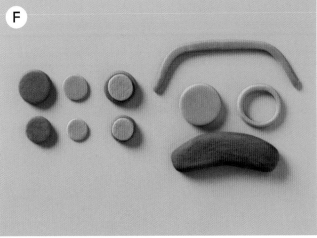

F

Tip

The instructions given are for a right hand drive car. If you are making a left hand drive car (Europe and America), reverse the instructions for the steering wheel and the driver's arm positions.

The driver

1 For the body roll 28g (1oz) of dark green sugarpaste into a cone shape (**G**). Place the cone inside the car behind the steering wheel and push a piece of dry spaghetti down through the centre, leaving 1cm (⅜in) showing at the top.

2 For the arms roll the remaining 20g (¾oz) of dark green sugarpaste into a sausage shape and divide in the centre with a diagonal cut (**G**). Bend the right arm at the elbow and attach to the top of the body, resting the forearm on the side of the car. Attach the left arm, but secure it to the back of the seat, allowing the end of the arm to rest on the other side of the car. Push a short piece of dry spaghetti into the end of each arm.

3 Make two hands by equally dividing 3g (⅛oz) of flesh-coloured sugarpaste. Make the hands as described on page 16 (**G**). Push the finished hands over the spaghetti at the wrists, place the right hand on the steering wheel and the left hand on the side of the car.

4 For the head take 25g (⅞oz) of flesh-coloured sugarpaste and roll into an oval shape. Pull down the neck at the base of the shape using a gentle twisting motion, cut off the excess and set aside to make the nose, ears and bottom lip.

5 For the mouth pull down the chin area, and then using tool no.11, mark a smile. Keep the top line of the smile straight and open the lower curve using the soft end of your paintbrush. Place a tiny cone shape of pink sugarpaste into the mouth for the tongue, then add a tiny banana shape in flesh for the bottom lip (**G**).

6 For the nose roll a small cone shape in flesh and attach in the centre of the face, using tool no.5 to make two holes for the nostrils (**G**).

7 For the eyes add two small white balls, placing them just above and on either side of the nose. Add two much smaller dark green balls for the pupils. Using tool no.4, mark lines on the face as shown (**G**).

8 For the ears add two small cone shapes in flesh and indent with the end of your paintbrush (**G**). Add some edible glue to the top of the body and push the head over the spaghetti.

9 For the hair take 2g (⅛oz) of grey sugarpaste and soften with white vegetable fat (shortening). Fill the cup of the sugar press (or garlic press), and squeeze out very short strands. Using tool no.4, slice off the strands and attach them around the ears and the back of the head, leaving the top bald. Roll a small sausage shape for the moustache, secure under the nose and mark with tool no.4 (**G**).

10 For the cap you will need 13g (½oz) of dark brown sugarpaste, taking off 12g (just under ½oz) for the crown. Roll into a ball and flatten, then slightly hollow out the underside with your fingers to fit the shape of the head. Finally, roll out the remaining dark brown sugarpaste and cut out a 2.5cm (1in) circle for the peak. Take out two-thirds with the same cutter to leave the correct shape (**G**). Attach to the underside of the cap. Apply edible glue to the head and attach the cap securely.

11 Make the scarf using 14g (½oz) of red sugarpaste rolled into a strip measuring 2 x 12cm (¾ x 4¾in). Using tool no.4, make the fringe by cutting vertical lines at each end. Take tool no.12 and add three rows of stitch marks (**G**). Gently fold the scarf and attach with edible glue around the neck and over the back of the seat.

The dog . . . .

1 To complete the dog you will need 45g (1½oz) of light brown sugarpaste. For the body take off 20g (¾oz) and roll into a tall cone shape (**H**). Push a piece of dry spaghetti through the centre, leaving 1cm (⅜in) showing at the top.

2 Make one back leg only using 3g (⅛oz) rolled into a soft cone shape. Narrow it at the ankle, keeping the upper part of the leg rounded (**H**). Mark the paw using tool no.4 and attach to the body. Place beside the driver in an upright position.

3 For the left front leg take off 2g (⅛oz) and roll into a sausage shape. Turn up the end for the foot and cut to a length of 3cm (1¼in). Turn the leg over onto its side and then make a diagonal cut across the back to reduce the bulk. Mark the paw using tool no.4 (**H**). Attach the leg to the body of the dog, resting the paw on the dashboard.

4 For the right front leg take off 2g (⅛oz) and roll into a very short sausage shape and mark the paw as before. Attach to the other side of the body, which is barely seen.

5 Make the tail by taking off 2g (⅛oz) and rolling into a tapered cone shape. Make a diagonal cut at the thickest end and attach to the back of the dog (**H**). Drape the tail over the top of the driver's hand.

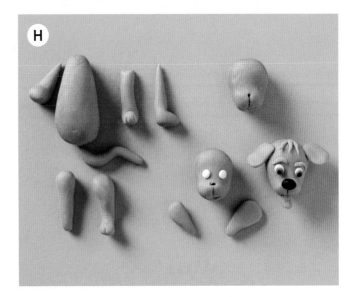

6 For the head take off 11g (⅜oz) and roll into a ball, place the ball into the palm of your hand and with the little finger of your other hand, indent the eye area (**H**). Flatten the front of the snout and, using tool no.4, mark a vertical line three-quarters of the way down from the top. Mark the smile using tool no.11 then open it up with the soft end of your paintbrush. Roll 1g (⅛oz) of pink sugarpaste into a tiny cone for the tongue and insert it into the mouth. Using tool no.5, make a hole at the top of the centre line and insert a tiny cone of black sugarpaste for the nose (**H**).

7 For the eyes roll two small balls of white sugarpaste. Attach just above the snout, add two small balls of light brown sugarpaste on the top and two even smaller balls of black sugarpaste for the pupils. Add a small eyebrow over each eye by rolling a small banana shape in light brown (**H**).

Tip

Flatten all the balls for the eyes with your finger to prevent them protruding.

8 For the ears take off 3g (⅛oz) of the light brown sugarpaste and divide equally. Roll into two soft cone shapes and flatten slightly. Attach to each side of the head in an upright position, securing with tool no.1 and then bring the ear forwards (**H**).

9 For the hair add three tapered cone shapes of light brown sugarpaste and attach to the top of the head (**H**). Slip the completed head over the spaghetti at the neck. Attach the end of the tongue to the side of the driver's face. Secure the windscreen to the front of the car being very careful not to bend it.

The orange car

1 Make the small cars using the Wilton mini egg pans and the recipe on page 21. Sandwich together the two halves with a thin layer of buttercream or your favourite filling then prepare the cakes as desired (see page 26).

2 To complete the orange car you will need 59g (2oz) of orange sugarpaste, 18g (¾oz) of black and 5g (¼oz) of grey. Roll out the orange sugarpaste and cover the cake completely, trimming it neatly and smoothing out any creases. Set the leftover paste aside.

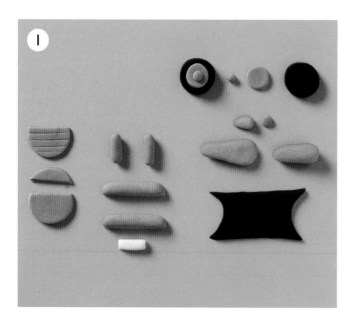

3 For the wheels roll out 12g (½oz) of black sugarpaste to a 5mm (⅛in) thickness and cut out four circles using a 2cm (¾in) round cutter. Thinly roll out 2g (⅛oz) of grey sugarpaste and cut out four 1.5cm (½in) circles to make the wheel trims. Attach to the centre of each wheel and add a small ball of grey to the centre (**I**). Insert a short piece of dry spaghetti into the car where the wheels are to be positioned, and then slip the wheels into place.

> *Tip*
>
> *The car should rest on the cake board – the wheels should not be supporting it.*

4 To make the wheel arches (fenders) take off 12g (½oz) of the orange sugarpaste, equally divide into four and roll into cone shapes. Slightly flatten with your finger and then arch the shape. Attach over each wheel. Roll a small cone shape in orange sugarpaste for the side (parking) lights. Add a small ball of grey to the front of each light, and one to the back of each wheel arch (fender) for the brake lights (**I**).

5 To complete the bumpers you will need 2g (⅛oz) of grey sugarpaste, take off two small balls, roll into short sausage shapes and set aside. Roll the remainder into a sausage shape 2.5cm (1in) long and cut in half lengthwise (**I**). Attach one half to the front of the car and one to the back. Attach the two small sausage shapes vertically over the back bumper.

6 Make the grill for the front of the car using 1g (⅛oz) of the grey sugarpaste. Cut out a 2.5cm (1in) circle, take off one-third and mark with lines using tool no.4 (**I**). Attach to the centre front of the car and over the front bumper.

7 For the roof roll out 6g (¼oz) of the black sugarpaste into a rectangle measuring 5 x 2.5cm (2 x 1in). Using a 2.5cm (1in) round cutter, take out a semi-circle at each end (**I**) and attach to the top of the car.

8 To finish the car use tool no.4 to mark vertical lines down both sides to show the divisions for the doors and windows. Lightly press the edge of a 2.5cm (1in) round cutter across the front to mark the windscreen (windshield) and do the same at the back for the rear window. Cut out a small rectangle measuring 5mm x 1cm (⅛ x ⅜in) from 1g (⅛oz) of white sugarpaste for the number (license) plate and secure under the front bumper. Dust the lights and grill with silver metallic dust food colour and the bumpers with pearl lustre dust food colour.

The other cars

1 **To complete the red car** you will need 65g (2¼oz) of red sugarpaste, 12g (½oz) of black and 5g (¼oz) of grey. Make as described for the orange car but make the roof in red.

2 **To complete the blue car** you will need 65g (2¼oz) of blue sugarpaste, 12g (½oz) of black and 5g (¼oz) of grey. Make as described for the orange car but make the roof in blue.

3 **To complete the yellow car** you will need 59g (2oz) of yellow sugarpaste, 12g (½oz) of black and 11g (½oz) of grey. Make as described for the orange car but make the roof in grey.

4 **Attach the four completed cars** around the cake board with strong edible glue (see page 24) in the desired positions. Finally, secure the large car in position on the top of the cake.

A Little More Fun!

Womanly Wheels

You could also make this cake for a lady car-fanatic's birthday using a female driver, cars in hot pink, purple and lime and cute white hearts instead of radiator grills. Try experimenting with go-faster stripes too! Why not make some extra cars to give to the party guests to take home? The Wilton mini egg pan (see Suppliers, page 126) will make four cars using the recipe on page 21.

The Toy Box

Childhood is such a special, magical time and no object embodies it more than a brightly coloured toy box full of treasured toys. The cute characters on this cake make it irresistible to children and a real thrill to receive for a birthday. You will have to dismantle the box to eat the cake, but that's all part of the fun!

"Quit clowning around and get on with cutting the cake!"

You will need

Sugarpaste

* 1kg 292g (2lb 13½oz) red
* 920g (2lb ½oz) white
* 600g (1lb 5oz) yellow
* 400g (14oz) blue
* 352g (12½oz) green
* 246g (8⅝oz) light brown
* 205g (7¼oz) flesh
* 86g (3oz) pink
* 80g (2⅞oz) orange
* 32g (1oz) black

Materials

* 30 x 20cm (12 x 8in) cake
* Pink food colour pen
* Dust food colour in red, pink and pink sparkle
* Brown liquid food colour
* Paste food colour in purple and rose pink
* 5 portions of pastillage (see recipe, page 23)
* White vegetable fat (shortening)
* Edible glue (see page 24)

Equipment

* 46 x 40cm (18 x 16in) cake drum
* Balloons textured rolling pin
* 5cm (2in), 4cm (1½in), 3cm (1¼in), 2.5cm (1in), 1.5cm (½in), 13mm (½in), 1cm (⅜in) and 5mm (⅛in) round cutters
* 3cm (1¼in) and 2cm (¾in) triangle cutters
* 5cm (2in) and 3cm (1¼in) square cutter
* 1.5cm (½in) star cutter
* 4cm (1½in) pastry cutter
* 6 white flower stamens
* Red ribbon 15mm (½in) wide x 190cm (75in) long
* Non-toxic glue
* Basic tool kit (see pages 10–12)

Making the toy box . . . .

1 For the front take one portion of the pastillage, coloured with red dust food colour, and roll out to an even 6mm (¼in) thickness. Using a cutting wheel (or pizza cutter) cut out a rectangle measuring 33 x 13cm (13 x 5in). Set aside on a flat surface dusted with icing (confectioners') sugar to prevent it sticking.

2 Mark the lines across the front before it hardens off using the edge of a ruler. Leave to harden for 12 hours, then carefully turn it over and leave for a further 12 hours.

Tip

Pastillage cracks very easily so be careful not to bend it. When it is thoroughly dry, sand down any rough edges with fine sandpaper.

3 For the side roll out another portion of red pastillage to an even 6mm (¼in) thickness and cut out a rectangle measuring 23 x 13cm (9 x 5in). Place on a flat surface and mark with a ruler as before. Make two and set aside. Keep any leftover pastillage tightly wrapped in a freezer bag in the fridge – you will need some later for the box corners.

4 For the lid cut out two pieces of cardboard measuring 33 x 36cm (13 x 14in) to support the structure as it dries at an angle. Combine two portions of red pastillage and roll out to an even 6mm (¼in) thickness. Cut out a rectangle measuring 33 x 36cm (13 x 14in). Mark the surface with lines as before. Slide one piece of card underneath the lid and place the other piece on the top; it is now sandwiched between the two cards to keep it flat, so that you can turn it over and then remove the top card. Elevate the top edge of the lid by stacking two 5mm (⅛in) wooden spacing rods on top of each other and sliding them underneath the card to support the edge. Leave to dry for a minimum of 24 hours before turning over. When ready to turn over, remove the pastillage piece from the card carefully and replace the card on the underside. Support as before.

Covering the board

1 Place the upturned cake tin on top of the board and mark around it to indicate the size of the cake. Offset it to the back of the board, leaving room at the front for the figures.

2 To cover the board you will need 400g (14oz) of yellow sugarpaste. Roll out four strips to an even 3mm (⅛in) thickness to go around each side of the board. Roll over with the textured rolling pin to decorate. Moisten the edge of the board with cooled boiled water. Make a straight edge on each strip and place this on the marked line. Overlap the strip at each end and make a diagonal cut through both thicknesses on each corner. Remove the excess from the top and underneath to make a perfect join. Trim the edges with a marzipan knife and set the board aside to dry. Edge the board with the red ribbon, securing it with non-toxic glue.

Covering the cake

1 To cover the cake you will need 1kg 200g (2lb 10¼oz) of red sugarpaste rolled out to an even 5mm (⅛in) thickness. Cover the cake in the usual way (see pages 26–27) then place on the board inside the allocated space.

2 Make some extra-strong glue by mixing some red sugarpaste with edible glue to a stiff paste. Apply the glue to the sides of the cake. Attach the dry pastillage pieces to the front and sides of the cake, keeping them very straight, then attach the back with the lid.

3 To make the corner supports roll out 100g (3½oz) of the leftover red pastillage and cut four pieces measuring 4 x 13cm (1½ x 5in). Attach to each corner for extra support and use tool no.12 to mark stitches down each edge. Equally divide 3g (⅛oz) of the red pastillage, shape into two small triangles and attach one to each of the front corners to neaten them.

Decorating the box

1 Make some bunting to go across the back of the box lid using 15g (½oz) of white sugarpaste rolled into a lace 36cm (14in) long. Flatten the lace slightly with your rolling pin and attach across the back of the lid (**A**).

2 To make the flags you will need 15g (½oz) each of red, blue, green and yellow sugarpaste. Roll out and cut three 3cm (1¼in) triangles in each colour and secure to the lace with edible glue (**A**).

3 For the string of bunting on the front of the box you will need 2g (1/16oz) of white sugarpaste rolled to a length of 16cm (6¼in). Flatten with your rolling pin then cut out the flags using a 2cm (¾in) triangle cutter. Secure to the centre front of the toy box with edible glue.

Tip
Model your toys on a cake card before lifting them onto the cake.

The clown's ball

Make this well in advance so that it will harden before the clown is made. Take 200g (7oz) of white sugarpaste and roll into a perfectly round ball. Decorate the front of the ball with stars using 12g (½oz) of blue sugarpaste and a 1.5cm (½in) star cutter. Set aside to harden.

The teddy bears

1 To complete both bears you will need 238g (8⅜oz) of light brown sugarpaste. Take off 45g (1½oz) for the body and roll into a cone shape (**B**). Push a piece of dry spaghetti down through the body, leaving 2cm (¾in) showing at the top. Place at the front of the toy box.

2 For the legs take off 20g (¾oz) and roll into a sausage shape. Turn up at each end to form the feet. Make a diagonal cut at the top of each leg and then glue them to the base of the cone inside the box (**B**).

3 For the arms take off 18g (¾oz) and roll into a short sausage shape, making a diagonal cut at the top. Attach to the cone and secure over the edge of the box. Mark the paws using tool no.4 (**B**).

4 For the head roll 30g (1oz) into a smooth ball. Take off a further 4g (⅛oz), roll into an oval shape and attach to the front of the head. Using tool no.4, mark a line down the centre of the muzzle and mark a smile at the base of the line on either side, using tool no.11 (**B**).

5 To make the eyes equally divide 0.5g (⅛oz) of white sugarpaste and roll into two small balls then add a tiny ball of black on the top of each and flatten with your finger (**B**).

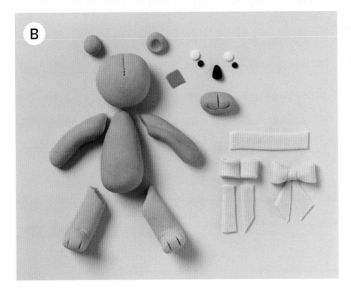

6 To make the ears equally divide 2g (⅛oz) of the light brown sugarpaste and roll into two balls. Attach to each side of the head and indent with tool no.1 (**B**). Make two bears.

7 To make the bow roll out 3g (⅛oz) of pink sugarpaste into a rectangle measuring 14mm x 3cm (½ x 1¼in). Cut the strip in half lengthwise. Take one strip and turn the ends into the centre leaving two loops. Cut the second strip in half lengthwise to make the tails. Make a diagonal cut at the end of each tail. Make a further diagonal cut lengthwise to taper the tails (**B**). Attach to the top of the bear's head. Decorate with dots using a pink food colour pen.

8 Add a small blue patch to the other bear's head by rolling out 0.5g (⅛oz) of blue sugarpaste and cutting a 1cm (⅜in) square patch using tool no.4. Glue in place then using the fine end of tool no.12, mark around the edges with stitch marks (**B**).

The caterpillar

1 For the body take 50g (1¾oz) of pink sugarpaste and 40g (1½oz) each of orange, yellow and blue and roll each colour into a smooth ball, then set aside to harden. Take a length of dry spaghetti to go through the balls and stack them one on top of the other in the following order: pink, orange, blue and yellow (**C**). Leave 3cm (1¼in) of dry spaghetti showing at the top to support the head.

2 To make the legs and feet you will need 5g (¼oz) each of pink, orange, blue and yellow sugarpaste equally divided. Make a cone shape and turn up the widest end, then slightly flatten with your finger. Push a piece of dry spaghetti into the narrow end and push into the side of the body, mixing up the colours as shown (**C**).

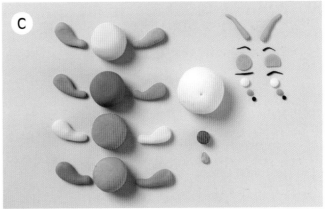

3 For the head roll 50g (1¾oz) of white sugarpaste into a smooth ball. Push a short piece of dry spaghetti into the centre of the face. Roll 0.5g (⅛oz) of red sugarpaste into a ball for the nose and slip it over the spaghetti. Push the end of your paintbrush below the nose to make a hole for the mouth. Roll 0.5g (⅛oz) of pink sugarpaste into a small cone shape for the tongue and glue it inside the hole. Mark the tongue down the centre with tool no.4 (**C**).

4 To make the eyes roll two small balls of white sugarpaste and place them just above and on either side of the nose. Add two much smaller balls of blue sugarpaste on top for the irises, slightly flatten with your finger, and finally add two tiny balls of black on top for the pupils (**C**).

5 For the eyelids roll out 2g (⅛oz) of green sugarpaste and cut out two 1cm (⅜in) circles. Take off one-third of each to make half-moon shapes and attach over the eyes. Set the leftover green sugarpaste aside for the antennae. To outline the eyes, roll a sliver of black sugarpaste and glue to the base of each eyelid. Add two further slivers of black sugarpaste for the eyebrows (**C**).

6 For the antennae roll the leftover green sugarpaste into a sausage shape and taper at one end (**C**). Gently push a piece of dry spaghetti into the fat end, leaving 1cm (⅜in) showing at the base. Push this into each side of the head. Dust the cheeks with pink dust food colour. Secure the caterpillar to the centre back of the toy box.

The train

1 To make the chassis of the train take 50g (1¾oz) of blue sugarpaste and roll into a rectangular prism measuring 3cm (1¼in) high x 9cm (3½in) wide x 1cm (⅜in) deep (**D**).

2 For the boiler roll 23g (⅞oz) of red sugarpaste and 23g (⅞oz) of yellow into a short sausage shape. Attach together on top of the chassis. Take 8g (¼oz) of red sugarpaste, shape into a cube and place at the back of the chassis (**D**).

3 Add the cab using 13g (½oz) of blue sugarpaste shaped into a square and attached to the red cube. Cut out a small square for the roof using 3g (⅛oz) of blue sugarpaste and attach to the top of the cab (**D**).

4 To make the funnel roll 5g (¼oz) of blue sugarpaste into a short sausage shape and attach to the top of the boiler. Add a small flattened ball of yellow sugarpaste to the top. Decorate the train with some circles made by rolling 1g (⅛oz) of black sugarpaste into small balls then flattening them with your finger (**D**).

5 Make the wheels using 36g (1¼oz) of green sugarpaste divided equally into four. Roll into balls and press with your finger to flatten. Take 2g (⅛oz) of yellow sugarpaste, divide equally into four, roll into balls, flatten with your finger and attach to the centre of each wheel (**D**). Secure two wheels to each side of the chassis. Place the train to the left of the caterpillar inside the toy box.

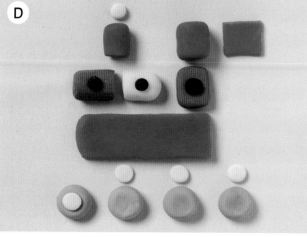

Tip

When rolling out sugarpaste, use wooden spacing rods (see page 10) to ensure an even thickness.

The boy doll ....

1 For the body roll 100g (3½oz) of blue sugarpaste into a carrot shape, turning the shape so that the thinnest end is at the top, then slightly flatten the shape by smoothing it with your hand. Take tool no.4 and make a division in the thickest end to form the shorts. Soften and round off all the edges then bend the figure into a sitting position. Push a piece of dry spaghetti down through the centre, leaving 2cm (¾in) showing at the top. Hollow out the knee areas using the ball end of tool no.3 (**E**). Push a piece of dry spaghetti into each of the holes to support the legs.

2 Make the shoes using 8g (¼oz) of white sugarpaste equally divided. Roll into two short sausage shapes. To form the soles, equally divide 2g (⅛oz) of black sugarpaste and roll into two thinner sausage shapes, then flatten with your fingers. Attach to the base of the shoes and mark the heels across with tool no.4 (**E**). Set the shoes aside.

3 For the legs equally divide 27g (1oz) of flesh-coloured sugarpaste and roll into two sausage shapes, making a straight cut at the top of each (**E**). Bend to form the knees and slip the legs over the spaghetti inside the trousers. Add a short piece of dry spaghetti to the other end of the legs. Attach the shoes and arrange into position.

4 Make a trouser pocket using 1g (⅛oz) of blue sugarpaste. Cut out a 1cm (⅜in) square using tool no.4 and stitch mark on three sides using tool no.12 (**E**). Attach to the right trouser leg with edible glue.

5 For the socks roll out 3g (⅛oz) of white sugarpaste into a rectangle measuring 2 x 3.5cm (¾ x 1⅜in). Fold over the top of the shape to form the sock (**E**). Make two and attach one over the join of each leg and shoe.

6 To make the T-shirt roll out 22g (¾oz) of yellow sugarpaste. Cut out two 5cm (2in) squares and make a diagonal cut at each top corner (**E**). Apply some edible glue around the top and sides of the body and place one square at the back, bringing it around to the side. Using tool no.4, make a straight line on each side seam, removing any excess sugarpaste. Place the second square to the front of the body and trim the side seams as before to make a neat join. Push a piece of dry spaghetti into each shoulder.

7 For the sleeves equally divide 20g (¾oz) of yellow sugarpaste, roll into two cone shapes and hollow out using tool no.3 (**E**). Slip over the spaghetti at the shoulders and push a piece of dry spaghetti into the end of each sleeve.

8 For the arms roll 20g (¾oz) of flesh-coloured sugarpaste into a sausage shape. Make a straight cut in the centre and lightly press the rounded ends with your finger. Using tool no.4, mark the thumbs and move them away from the hands, rounding them off. Indent four fingers on each hand and narrow at the wrists (**E**). Slip the arms over the spaghetti inside the sleeves.

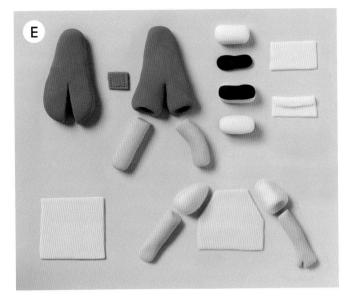

E

9 To make the head roll 30g (1oz) of flesh-coloured sugarpaste into a ball, pull down the neck and indent the eye area (see page 14). Make a straight cut at the base of the neck. Use the paste you have cut off to make the nose and ears. Roll a small ball into an oval shape for the nose and place in the centre of the face. Using tool no.11, mark a smile under the nose. Open the mouth with the soft end of your paintbrush and attach a tiny banana shape for the bottom lip (**F**).

10 For the eyes roll two small balls of white sugarpaste then add a tiny ball of blue on the top of each, and finally add a dot of black for the pupils (**F**). Dust the cheeks with a dry brush and some pink dust food colour.

11 For the ears roll two small cone shapes, attach to the head and indent with the end of your paintbrush (**F**).

12 For the hair soften 5g (¼oz) of light brown sugarpaste with white vegetable fat (shortening) and fill the cup of a sugar press (or garlic press). Squeeze out strands of hair and arrange over the head securing with edible glue (**F**).

13 To make the hat roll 15g (½oz) of blue sugarpaste into a cone shape. Using tool no.3, hollow out the wide end and attach to the head. Roll out the blue sugarpaste left over from the body, cut a strip measuring 1 x 10cm (⅜ x 4in) and mark with tool no.12. Soften 3g (⅛oz) of yellow sugarpaste with white vegetable fat (shortening) and using the sugar press (or garlic press), extrude short strands, pinch together and secure to the top (**F**). Place the boy doll on the left-hand side of the toy box.

Tip
When extruding the hair, take off one layer at a time rather than clumps.

The girl doll

1 Make the lower body and upper legs in one piece by taking 65g (2¼oz) of blue sugarpaste and rolling into a carrot shape. Turn the shape over so that the thickest part is at the bottom and shape as for the boy doll, except that this piece finishes at the waistline (**G**). Place the body into a sitting position.

2 Make the shoes using 10g (⅜oz) of green sugarpaste equally divided, and roll as for the boy doll's shoes (see page 59). Add the soles using 4g (⅛oz) of white sugarpaste equally divided, mark the heels with tool no.4 and set aside (**G**).

3 For the lower legs equally divide 12g (½oz) of flesh-coloured sugarpaste and roll into a sausage shape 8cm (3in) long. Cut the sausage in half making two legs (**G**). Push a short piece of dry spaghetti into the end of each trouser leg then slip the legs over the top. Push another short piece of dry spaghetti into the bottom of each leg and attach the shoes.

4 For the socks roll out 3g (⅛oz) of pink sugarpaste into a rectangle measuring 3.5 x 2cm (1⅜ x ¾in). Fold over the top of the shape to form the sock (**G**). Make two and attach one over the join of each leg and shoe.

5 Make the upper body using 30g (1oz) of flesh-coloured sugarpaste rolled into a cone shape. With the thickest part of the cone at the top, shape the neck by pinching up from the centre. Shape the shoulders and cut off at the waist (**G**). Attach the upper and lower body together and push a piece of dry spaghetti down through the neck into the base of the body, leaving 2cm (¾in) showing to support the head. Push a piece of dry spaghetti into each shoulder.

6 For the arms roll 20g (¾oz) of flesh-coloured sugarpaste into a sausage shape and make a diagonal cut in the centre. Narrow at the wrists and slightly flatten the ends to form the hands. Indent each hand as described for the boy doll (see page 59) (**G**). Attach the arms to the top of the shoulders over the spaghetti.

7 To make the vest randomly mix together 12g (½oz) of pink sugarpaste and 12g (½oz) of orange. Roll out the marbled paste and cut a rectangle for the front measuring 7 x 5cm (2¾ x 2in), taking out a 3cm (1¼in) square at the top (**G**). Attach this piece to the front of the doll, taking the straps over the shoulders.

8 For the back of the vest cut out a rectangle measuring 7.5 x 5.5cm (3 x 2⅛in). Take out a 3cm (1¼in) square at the top (**G**) and place at the back of the doll, bringing the longer straps forwards over the shoulders. The side edges should line up with each other to make a perfect join.

9 For the buttons roll out 1g (⅛oz) of green sugarpaste, cut two 1cm (⅜in) circles then indent the centres with a 5mm (⅛in) round cutter. Place on the ends of the straps and mark the holes with tool no.5 (**G**).

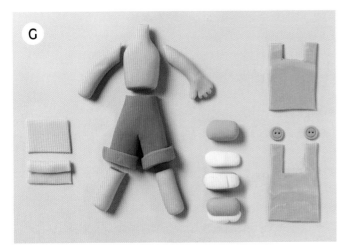

G

10 For the head roll 30g (1oz) of flesh-coloured sugarpaste into a smooth ball and indent the eye area as before. Pinch out the nose and shape further using the soft end of your paintbrush. Add two nostrils using tool no.5. Mark the mouth by pushing the end of your paintbrush into the paste and pulling it down to open (**H**).

11 For the eyes roll two small cone shapes in white sugarpaste, add a smaller cone shape on the top of each in blue, and place a tiny black cone shape on the top to finish (**H**). Paint around the eyes and add the eyelashes using some brown liquid food colour and a no.0000 paintbrush. Dust the cheeks with pink dust food colour and a dry brush. Attach the head over the spaghetti at the neck.

12 To create the hairstyle mix together 12g (½oz) of white sugarpaste with 3g (⅛oz) of light brown. Take off 12g (½oz) and roll into a ball, then shape it with your thumb and finger to fit over the doll's head like a cap. Using tool no.4, mark a parting from the front down to the hairline at the back then mark lines for the hair from the edges to the parting. To make the ringlets, soften the remainder of the sugarpaste with some white vegetable fat (shortening), fill the cup of the sugar press (or garlic press) and extrude some lengths of hair. Take off three at a time and twist together. Add to the side and front of the head (**H**).

13 For the bow roll out 4g (¼oz) of white sugarpaste and make two small white bows as described for the teddy bear (see page 57) but without the bow tails (**H**). Position the doll inside the toy box on the right-hand side at the back.

The purple dinosaur

1 Make the purple sugarpaste by colouring 285g (10oz) of white sugarpaste with purple paste food colour. Take off 200g (7oz) to make the body and neck. Shape into a fat cone and then pull out the pointed end to make the tail and shape the body. Pull out the neck and roll it into shape (**I**). Push a piece of dry spaghetti down into the neck, leaving 2cm (¾in) showing to support the head.

2 Make the back legs by rolling 32g (1oz) into a sausage shape and cut in half. Turn up each end to form the feet then make a diagonal cut across the top (**I**). Attach to the back of the body.

3 For the front legs take off 24g (⅞oz), roll into a sausage shape and cut in half. Push up the rounded ends to form the feet and then make a diagonal cut across the top of each leg. Attach to the front of the body (**I**).

4 To make the pads and claws you will need 2g (⅛oz) of yellow sugarpaste. Make six thin cone shapes for the claws and roll the remaining sugarpaste into four balls of equal size. Press a pad onto the base of each foot then add the claws (**I**).

5 For the chest roll 15g (½oz) of yellow sugarpaste into a sausage shape and narrow it at the top (**I**). Attach to the front of the body and neck area.

6 For the head roll 26g (1oz) of the purple sugarpaste into a ball. Narrow half of the ball to form the snout, then shape a bump at the top for the forehead. Pinch out the side of the face and continue to mould until you are happy with the shape. Flatten the front of the snout and add two nostrils using tool no.5 (**I**).

7 Make the lower jaw using 3g (⅛oz) of yellow sugarpaste rolled into a soft cone shape and then flatten with your finger (**I**). Attach this underneath the snout, leaving the front open. Slip the head over the spaghetti at the neck and secure with edible glue.

8 Create the eyes using two small balls of white sugarpaste, press onto the face, then add two small balls of black sugarpaste for the pupils. Roll a thin lace of black sugarpaste for the eyebrows and attach over the eyes (**I**).

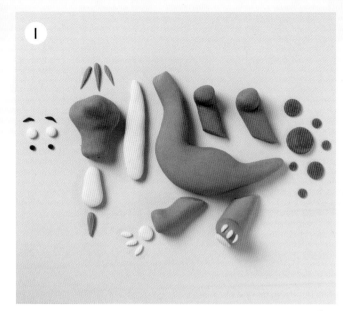

9 To make the spots, hair and tongue add some rose pink paste food colour to 3g (⅛oz) of white sugarpaste. Take off a small amount and roll three long cone shapes for the hair. Attach on the top of the head. Roll a small cone shape for the tongue, place inside the mouth and mark with tool no.4. Take the remaining pink sugarpaste and roll into four small, two medium and one large ball, flatten them with your finger and attach to the back of the dinosaur with edible glue (**I**). Secure the figure in the centre of the toy box.

The rabbit

1 For the body roll 100g (3½oz) of white sugarpaste into a cone shape then use tool no.12 to run a line of stitch marks down the centre front (**J**). Push a piece of dry spaghetti down through the centre, leaving 3cm (1¼in) showing at the top to take the head.

2 For the feet equally divide 30g (1oz) of white sugarpaste and roll into soft cone shapes. Push two short pieces of dry spaghetti into the base of the body and slip the feet over the top, turning them out slightly (**J**).

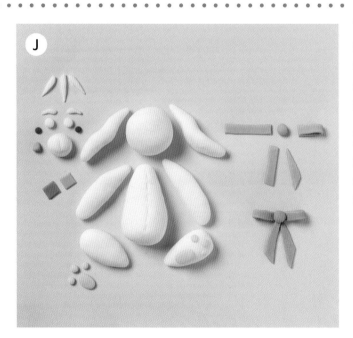

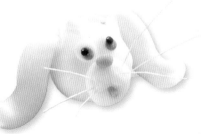

3 For the toes take 3g (⅛oz) of pink sugarpaste and roll six small flattened balls. Attach three to the top of each foot then add a larger flattened ball for the pad at the base of each foot (**J**).

4 To make the arms equally divide 40g (1½oz) of white sugarpaste and roll into two flattened cone shapes (**J**). Push a short piece of dry spaghetti into the shoulders and attach the arms, bringing them to the side of the body.

5 For the head take 40g (1½oz) of white sugarpaste and roll into a ball, slip over the spaghetti at the neck and secure with edible glue. Push a short piece of dry spaghetti into the centre front of the head then roll 6g (¼oz) of white sugarpaste into a ball for the muzzle. Slip this over the spaghetti and mark a line down the centre with tool no.4. Using tool no.11, mark a smile at the bottom of the line. Make a small cone shape of pink sugarpaste for the nose and attach at the top of the muzzle (**J**).

6 Make the eyes by rolling two small balls of white sugarpaste and attach just above and on either side of the nose. Add two tiny balls of blue sugarpaste for the pupils. Roll two eyebrows in white and attach over each eye (**J**).

7 To make the ears equally divide 30g (1oz) of white sugarpaste and roll into two soft cone shapes. Flatten each ear and attach to the side of the head. Using tool no.4, cut out a 1cm (⅜in) square of blue and pink for patches, stitch mark with tool no.12 and attach to the body (**J**).

8 For the whiskers take six flower stamens and cut off the ends, push three into each side of the face.

9 For the bow roll out 6g (¼oz) of pink sugarpaste and cut out a rectangle measuring 3 x 3.5cm (1¼ x 1⅜in). Cut into four equal strips, use two to form the loops and two for the tails, as described for the bow on the teddy bear (see page 57). Add a small ball in the centre to finish (**J**). Attach under the chin of the rabbit. Sit the rabbit in the right-hand front corner of the box.

The skateboard

1 For the board roll 40g (1½oz) of yellow sugarpaste into a sausage shape. Use a rolling pin to flatten the shape and widen it then turn up the ends and set aside to dry (**K**).

2 For the axles roll out 8g (¼oz) of black sugarpaste, and cut out two strips measuring 4cm x 5mm (1½ x ⅛in). Push a length of dry spaghetti through the centre, leaving a little showing to attach the wheels. Secure at the front and back on the underside of the board (**K**).

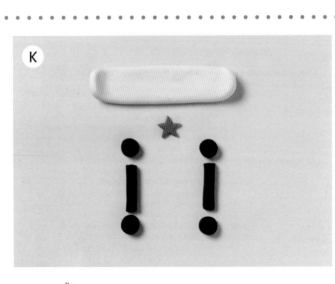

3 For the wheels roll out the remaining black sugarpaste and cut out four 13mm (½in) circles (**K**). Attach over the spaghetti on the axles and set aside to dry.

4 Make a star decoration using 1g (⅛oz) of red sugarpaste and a 1.5cm (½in) star cutter and secure with edible glue to the front of the skateboard (**K**). Secure the skateboard to the side of the boy doll.

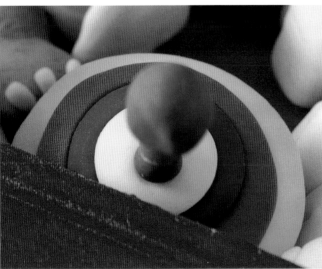

The spinning top

1 Take 60g (2oz) of blue sugarpaste and roll into a sphere shape (**L**). Place the sphere on top of a 4cm (1½in) pastry cutter while you add the design, this will keep it in shape.

2 Roll out 12g (½oz) of yellow sugarpaste and cut out a 5cm (2in) circle and then take out the centre with a 3cm (1¼in) round cutter. Set the 3cm (1¼in) circle aside to use for the top and place the ring around the widest part of the spinning top (**L**).

3 Roll out 10g (⅜oz) of red sugarpaste and cut out a 4cm (1½in) circle, take out the centre with a 2.5cm (1in) round cutter. Place the red ring on top of the yellow one. Using 8g (¼oz) of blue sugarpaste, cut out a 3cm (1¼in) circle and take out the centre using a 1.5cm (½in) round cutter. Place the blue ring above the red one and add the yellow circle on top (**L**).

4 To make the handle roll out 4g (⅛oz) of blue sugarpaste into a rectangle measuring 5 x 3cm (2 x 1¼in) and run a line of edible glue down the centre. Place a 6cm (2⅜in) length of dry spaghetti on to the strip and fold it over, trimming the sugarpaste close to the spaghetti. Roll the strip on the work surface to form a rod. Leave some of the dry spaghetti showing at the bottom and push it into the centre of the spinning top. Make a small ball from the leftover blue sugarpaste and attach it to the end of the handle (**L**). Place the completed spinning top at the front of the toy box, next to the rabbit.

The clown

1 Model the clown on top of the ball, but first push a long piece of dry spaghetti down through the centre of the ball, leaving 7cm (2¾in) showing at the top. Take 21g (¾oz) each of orange, yellow, white, and red sugarpaste and mix together randomly. To do this, break all the colours up into small balls and spread them out on the work surface. Gently bring them all together into one amount.

2 For the body take off 34g (1⅛oz) of the marbled sugarpaste and make a cone shape (**M**). Gently slide it over the spaghetti sticking out of the ball, so that he is balanced on the top. Push a short piece of dry spaghetti into the top to support the arms.

3 Make the legs by taking off 27g (1oz) and rolling into a sausage shape, then make a diagonal cut in the centre. Bend each leg at the knee and attach the diagonal cuts to the body, securing the legs to the ball (**M**). Push a short piece of dry spaghetti into the end of each leg.

4 To make the shoes equally divide 18g (¾oz) of black sugarpaste. Roll into two fat cone shapes, leaving the ends of the shoes very rounded. Attach the shoes firmly to the ends of the legs. Roll two small balls of red sugarpaste and secure one to the top of each shoe (**M**).

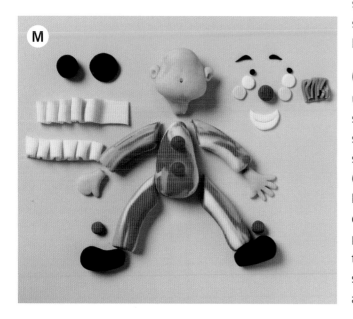

5 For the arms take 22g (¾oz) of the marbled sugarpaste and roll into a sausage shape. Make a diagonal cut in the centre and attach the arms to the top of the body (**M**). Bend the left arm at the elbow and push a piece of dry spaghetti into the wrist, through the arm and into the side of the body to hold it in position. Add a short piece of spaghetti into each wrist. Do not attach the right arm but keep it covered so that it will not dry out.

6 Make a white frill to go around the clown's neck using 12g (½oz) of white sugarpaste rolled out into a strip measuring 2 x 21cm (¾ x 8¼in). Hold the end of the strip with your left hand and as you pass the length of sugarpaste from your right hand, fold it gently into a frill (**M**). Once you have frilled the strip it should all be in your left hand. Place it down onto the work surface and spread out the folds. Press down one edge to hold the folds in place, leaving the other edge evenly frilled and loose. Trim the edge you have pressed down with tool no.4 to make it straight then attach it around the top of the body, leaving a space for the head in the centre.

7 For the head roll 30g (1oz) of flesh-coloured sugarpaste into a smooth ball. Pull down the neck and make a chin. Indent the eye area slightly and pinch out the cheeks. Slip the head over the spaghetti at the neck and turn it to the side. Roll a ball of red sugarpaste for the nose, push a short piece of spaghetti into the centre of the face and slip the nose over the top (**M**).

8 For the cheeks roll out 1g (¹⁄₁₆oz) of pink sugarpaste, cut out two 1cm (³⁄₈in) circles and attach on either side of the face. To make the mouth roll out a little of the white sugarpaste and cut out a 2cm (¾in) circle. Take out one-third of the circle to shape the smile, and then using the edge of the cutter, mark the centre to form two lips (**M**).

9 For the eyes cut out two 1cm (³⁄₈in) circles using 2g (¹⁄₁₆oz) of white sugarpaste and attach just above and on either side of the nose, then roll two small balls of black for the pupils and place them on top of the white circles. The eyes should be looking left. Roll two very thin laces for the eyebrows and attach in a curved shape over the eyes (**M**).

10 For the ears make two small balls in flesh and attach to the side of the face, indenting the centres with the end of your paintbrush (**M**).

11 For the hair soften 10g (³⁄₈oz) of green sugarpaste with white vegetable fat (shortening) and fill the cup of a sugar press (or garlic press). Extrude short strands of hair and chop them off in a clump with tool no.4 (**M**). Attach to the top of each ear and around the back of the head.

12 Make the hat using 8g (¼oz) of black sugarpaste. Take off 5g (¼oz) and cut out a 2cm (¾in) circle for the brim, then roll the remainder into a ball and attach to the top of the hat (**M**). Set aside.

13 For the hands equally divide 4g (¹⁄₈oz) of flesh-coloured sugarpaste and roll into two cone shapes. Make the hands as described on page 16 (**M**). Attach the right arm to the clown bending it up towards the head. Push a piece of dry spaghetti into each wrist and attach the hands.

14 Make two small frills for the cuffs by equally dividing 12g (½oz) of white sugarpaste and rolling out into two strips measuring 1.5 x 16cm (½ x 6¼in) (**M**). Frill the strips as described in step 6, opposite. Attach around each wrist.

15 Place the hat on top of the clown's head and secure the right hand to the brim. Secure the completed clown on the left of the board in front of the toy box.

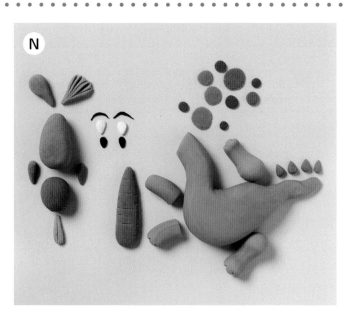

The green dinosaur

1 For the body and neck roll 215g (7½oz) of green sugarpaste into a cone shape, pull out the pointed end to form the tail and pinch along the top to make a ridge. To form the neck, pull out the paste at the widest part and lengthen it until the neck is long enough, being careful not to make it too thin (**N**). Push a piece of dry spaghetti down through the centre to support it, leaving 2cm (¾in) showing at the top.

2 Make up 30g (1oz) of purple sugarpaste by mixing white sugarpaste with some purple paste food colour. Take off 15g (½oz) and roll a sausage shape then taper it at the top. Flatten the shape with your finger keeping the edges nicely rounded. Attach to the front of the neck and mark across with lines using tool no.4 (**N**).

3 To make the back legs equally divide 26g (1oz) of green sugarpaste and roll into two balls. Narrow the centre of each ball to form the feet. Push a short piece of dry spaghetti into each hip and secure the legs to the body. Mark the claws with tool no.4 (**N**).

4 For the front legs equally divide 12g (½oz) of green sugarpaste and make two small sausage shapes. Push a short piece of dry spaghetti into each side of the dinosaur and slip the legs over the top, curving them downwards slightly, marking the claws with tool no.4 (**N**).

5 For the head roll 24g (⅞oz) of green sugarpaste into a cone shape. The narrow part of the cone will form the top of the head. For the snout, take 13g (½oz) of the purple sugarpaste and roll into an oval shape. Push a piece of dry spaghetti into the front of the head and attach the snout. Slightly flatten the front of the snout with your finger then mark two nostrils using tool no.5 (**N**).

6 For the mouth take a 3cm (1¼in) round cutter and push the edge into the paste, then open the mouth with the soft end of your paintbrush. Add two small cone shapes to the side of the snout by equally dividing 1g (⅛oz) of the purple sugarpaste – this will cover the join in between the head and the snout. Take 1g (⅛oz) of pink sugarpaste and roll into a cone shape to form the tongue. Attach inside the mouth, marking a line down the centre with tool no.4 (**N**).

7 For the eyes roll two small cones of white sugarpaste and position them just above the snout and not too far apart. Add two tiny cones of black sugarpaste for the pupils, then roll a very thin lace of black sugarpaste to outline the top of each eye (**N**).

8 Make a tuft of hair using 1g (⅛oz) of green sugarpaste rolled into a cone shape and flattened with your finger. Mark with tool no.4 and attach to the top of the head (**N**).

9 Make some spots to decorate the back of the dinosaur using 2g (⅛oz) of purple sugarpaste and 1g (⅛oz) of pink. Roll some small balls of purple sugarpaste and flatten them with your finger, then add some smaller pink spots on the top (**N**).

10 Decorate the ridge in the tail by making some small cone shapes from the remaining purple sugarpaste and attach along the length of the tail (**N**). Dust the spots with some pink sparkle dust food colour and a dry brush. Position the dinosaur on the on the right-hand side of the board in front of the toy box.

Tip
Paint some confectioners'
glaze on the eyes of your
characters to make them
sparkle with life.

A Little More Fun!

Teeny Toys

These mini toy boxes are made using Silverwood 6.5cm (2½in) square cake tins (see Suppliers, page 126), cutting each one in half to make two cakes. The cakes are then covered in sugarpaste pieces that have been textured with an FMM wood impression mat and left to dry completely before assembling. Your favourite toys from the main cake can then be placed inside each one ... which ones will you choose?

Retail Therapy

Her feet are hurting and her birthday money is spent,
but what is a girl to do when she just can't say no to
that last-minute must-have item? This pretty-in-pink
cake will be a real delight for any shopaholic mum,
daughter or friend and will make the ultimate
chic centrepiece to the birthday table.

"Decisions, decisions ... this one or that? I just love to shop!"

You will need

Sugarpaste

★ 2kg 400g (5lb 4⅝oz) pink
★ 290g (10¼oz) white
★ 270g (9½oz) black
★ 53g (1⅞oz) flesh

Materials

★ 20 x 7.5cm (8 x 3in) round cake
★ 20 x 5cm (8 x 2in) round cake
★ 6.5 x 5cm (2½ x 2in) round mini cake
★ Dust food colour in pale blue and pale pink
★ Black liquid food colour
★ White vegetable fat (shortening)
★ Confectioners' glaze
★ Edible glue (see page 24)
★ Non-toxic glue

Equipment

★ 30cm (12in) round cake drum
★ 20cm (8in) round cake card
★ 6.5cm (2½in) cake card
★ FMM brick impression mat
★ Straight-edged Garrett frill cutter
★ 3cm (1¼in) fleur-de-lis cutter
★ Small PME blossom cutter
★ 9cm (3½in), 8cm (3⅛in), 6cm (2⅜in), 3.5cm (1⅜in), 3cm (1¼in), 2cm (¾in), 1.5cm (½in), 13mm (½in) and 1cm (⅜in) round cutters
★ 1cm (⅜in) leaf cutter
★ 2.5cm (1in) and 1cm (⅜in) star cutters
★ 2cm (¾in), 1.5cm (½in) and 1cm (⅜in) square cutters
★ 2cm (¾in) diamond cutter
★ Pink ribbon 15mm (½in) wide x 1m (40in) long
★ Basic tool kit (see pages 10–12)

Covering the board and cakes

1 To cover the cakes and board you will need 1kg 600g (3lb 8½oz) of pink sugarpaste. Take off 500g (1lb 1½oz) and roll out to an even 3mm (⅛in) thickness. Cover the board in the usual way (see page 28) then trim the edges neatly with a marzipan knife.

2 To cover the two 20cm (8in) cakes take off 1kg 100g (2lb 6⅞oz) of the pink sugarpaste and roll out to an even 5mm (⅛in) thickness. Prepare the cakes then dowel and stack them (see page 29). Cover the stacked cakes with the sugarpaste in the usual way (see pages 26–27) then trim the edges neatly with a marzipan knife.

3 Attach the stacked cake to the centre of the board with strong edible glue (see page 24). Edge the board with the pink ribbon, securing it with non-toxic glue.

4 To cover the mini cake place onto a 6.5cm (2½in) cake card and prepare it as desired (see page 26). Roll out 160g (5⅝oz) of black sugarpaste and cover in the usual way. Roll out 16g (½oz) of pink sugarpaste and cut out five 1.5cm (½in), five 13mm (½in) and five 1cm (⅜in) circles. Glue the spots around the sides of the cake.

The shoe shop

1 For the large, central shop front roll out 150g (5¼oz) of pink sugarpaste to a 5mm (⅛in) thickness. Cut to measure 14 x 12cm (5½ x 4¾in). Place flat onto a cake card dusted with icing (confectioners') sugar to prevent it sticking.

2 For the brick pattern place the FMM brick impression mat horizontally across the sugarpaste about 4cm (1½in) from the top, and gently but evenly roll over the mat with your rolling pin. Carefully remove the mat and place it directly below the previously textured area, keeping the pattern correct. Repeat until you have covered the piece. Lightly mark the centre point at the top, and using a 6cm (2⅜in) round cutter, take out a curve evenly on each side of the mark to shape the top (**A**). Attach to the centre front of the cake with edible glue.

3 Make two side pillars using 60g (2oz) of pink sugarpaste rolled out to a 5mm (⅛in) thickness. Cut two strips measuring 8 x 2cm (3⅛ x ¾in). Using the edge of a ruler, mark each piece with straight vertical lines. Make a right or left diagonal cut at the top of each piece and attach to each side of the shop front (**A**).

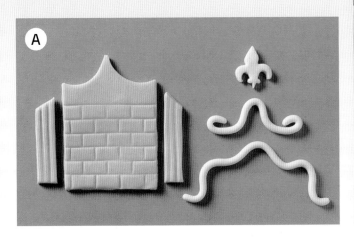

4 For the top pediment decoration you will need 13g (½oz) of white sugarpaste. Take off 6g (¼oz) and roll a thick lace 16cm (6¼in) long. Apply to the top of the shop and curl up at each end. Roll the remaining 7g (¼oz) of white into a lace 22cm (8⅝in) long and attach to the top, allowing the sides to hang down to the top of the brickwork, and then curl it upwards. Secure firmly with edible glue. Add the motif to the top using 8g (¼oz) of white sugarpaste and a 3cm (1¼in) fleur-de-lis cutter or any other pretty shape (**A**).

5 To make the shop window you will need 100g (3½oz) of pink sugarpaste. Roll out to a thickness of 5mm (⅛oz) then cut into a shape measuring 10 x 8cm (4 x 3⅛in). Using the brick impression mat, texture the bottom of the piece two rows high. Make the curve at the top using a 9cm (3½in) round cutter or the edge of a cake card (**B**). Place the piece flat onto a dusted cake card.

6 For the canopy you will need 40g (1½oz) of white sugarpaste. Roll out to a 3mm (⅛in) thickness and cut out an 8cm (3⅛in) circle. Take off one-third and set aside. Trim the edge of the canopy with a straight-edged Garrett frill cutter. Roll the remainder into a tapered sausage shape and place across the top of the window in a curve, securing with edible glue. Place the canopy over the top (**B**). Attach the window to the shop front.

7 To decorate the windowsill make a twist using 5g (¼oz) of white sugarpaste and 5g (¼oz) of pink. Begin by rolling each colour into a thin lace then twist them together evenly (**B**). Cut to a length of 10cm (4in) and attach to the cake. Make a strip to edge the whole shop window using 10g (⅜oz) of white sugarpaste and secure with edible glue.

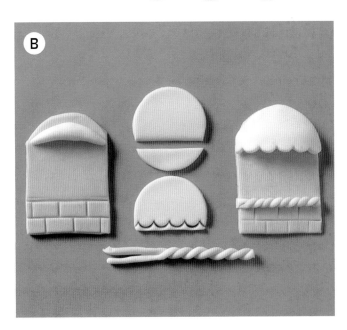

8 To make the hat and shoes in the window you will need 10g (⅜oz) of white sugarpaste rolled out thinly. For the hat, cut out a 1.5cm (½in) square. Using tool no.4, cut a diagonal line from the top corner to shape the top. Shape the brim into a curve by taking out a small amount from the bottom of the square with a 2cm (¾in) round cutter. Smooth the edges with your finger to soften. Add a small flower using a leftover amount of pink sugarpaste and a small blossom cutter and set aside (**C**).

9 For the shoe cut out a 2cm (¾in) square. Shape the top using tool no.4 then round off the toe. Mark the line of the wedge heel. Indent a platform sole and mark horizontal lines across the wedge. Add a bow to the shoe by rolling a tiny lace. Make two small loops, add a small ball in the centre and set aside (**C**).

10 For the boot cut out a 2cm (¾in) square and take out a small 'V' shape to mark the heel. Using a 2cm (¾in) round cutter, take out a curve at the front and a smaller curve at the back. Mark the sole with tool no.4, the eyelets with tool no.5, then mark a line of stitch marks with the fine end of tool no.12 to form the cuff. Add vertical lines to finish (**C**).

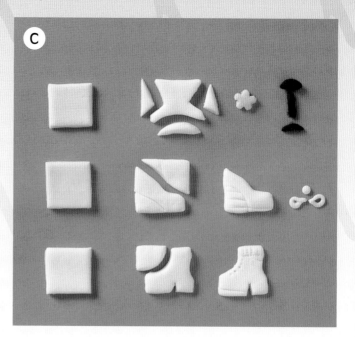

11 To make the hatstand roll a tiny amount of black sugarpaste into a small oval shape for the top and attach a short rolled lace for the upright. Make the base by rolling a curved sausage shape (**C**). Attach the hatstand to the centre of the window display with the hat on the top. Secure the shoe and the boot on either side.

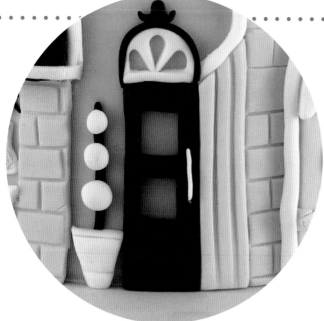

The black door and the plant

1 For the door roll out 20g (¾oz) of black sugarpaste to a 5mm (⅛in) thickness and cut a strip measuring 7 x 3cm (2¾ x 1¼in). Cut out two windows using a 1.5cm (½in) square cutter, and at the bottom of the door, indent the square using a 1cm (⅜in) square cutter (**D**). Attach the door to the left-hand side of the shop with edible glue.

2 To make the fan light roll out 5g (¼oz) of white sugarpaste and cut out a 3cm (1¼in) circle. Cut the circle in half, and using a 1cm (⅜in) leaf cutter, take out three shapes. Attach the fan light to the top of the door and edge it with 2g (⅛oz) of black sugarpaste rolled into a thin lace, making a swirl at the top. Roll a tiny sausage shape in white for the door handle and place in a vertical position on the side of the door (**D**).

3 Make the plant pot using 3g (⅛oz) of white sugarpaste and shape into a triangular shape. Secure to the side of the black door. Roll 1g (⅛oz) of black sugarpaste into a thin lace for the stem and place it in a vertical position in the centre of the pot. Using 1g (⅛oz) of white sugarpaste, roll three different sized balls and glue at intervals on the stem (**D**).

Tip

Because the cake is curved you must attach the shop fronts to to the cake before they dry out.

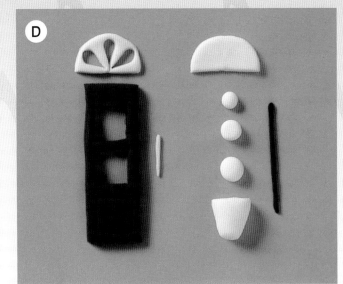

The clothes shop

1 For the shop front roll out 100g (3½oz) of pink sugarpaste and cut a piece measuring 10 x 12cm (4 x 4¾in). Texture with the brick impression mat and curve the top edge as before. Take out a 2 x 5cm (¾ x 2in) space for the window (**E**) and secure to the cake with edible glue.

2 For the window box roll out 8g (¼oz) of white sugarpaste and cut a strip measuring 1 x 10cm (⅜ x 4in). Make a diagonal cut at each end and mark with tool no.4 (**E**). Attach below the shop window with edible glue.

3 For the canopy you will need 35g (1¼oz) of black sugarpaste rolled out to a measurement of 5 x 12cm (2 x 4¾in) and shaped into a curve at the top. Roll a sausage shape using 15g (½oz) of pink sugarpaste and place over the top of the window to support the canopy. Apply edible glue to the top of the sausage and around the top of the shop front then carefully attach the canopy.

4 For the canopy decoration roll 7g (¼oz) of white sugarpaste into a thin sausage shape 22cm (8⅝in) long. Cut in half and secure to the top of the canopy, curling the ends at the centre. Roll out 6g (¼oz) of white sugarpaste and cut a 2cm (¾in) diamond then attach to the centre of the curls. Roll out 6g (¼oz) of white sugarpaste, cut out a narrow strip 17cm (6⅝in) long and apply to the bottom edge of the canopy. Cut out one 2.5cm (1in) star in white and one 1cm (⅜in) star in black (**E**). Glue the black star on top of the white and secure in the centre of the canopy.

5 To make all the clothing in the window you will need 8g (¼oz) of white sugarpaste, 1g (⅛oz) of black and 1g (⅛oz) of pink. Begin by rolling 1g (⅛oz) of black into a very fine lace. Cut into three 2.5cm (1cm) lengths for the stands (**F**) and glue inside the window.

6 Make the dress by cutting out a 2.5cm (1cm) square of thinly rolled out white sugarpaste. Cut away the arms using the corner of the cutter and make a diagonal cut on each side. Using the fine edge of tool no.12, add rows of stitch marks across and down the skirt. Add a tiny lace of pink for the tie (**F**). Attach the dress to the central clothes stand.

7 For the hat roll 1g (⅛oz) of white sugarpaste into a small cone shape and cut across the thickest part to make a straight edge. Add a row of stitch marks with tool no.12 (**F**) and then place it above the dress.

8 Shape the dungarees from a 1.5cm (½in) square of white sugarpaste and make a division for the legs. Taper the sides to the shoulder and then cut out a square for the neck leaving two shoulder straps. Add a line of stitch marks across the chest and the edge of the legs. Cut out a very small square of pink for a pocket, and add stitch marks to three sides. Add two small black balls for the buttons at the shoulder (**F**) and secure to the right-hand clothes stand.

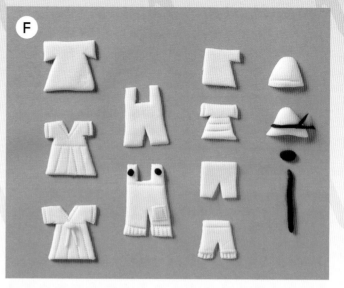

9 For the other hat make a cone shape in white sugarpaste and add a fine lace of black sugarpaste to trim (**F**). Attach above the dungarees.

10 For the two-piece set cut out two 13mm (½in) squares. On one square, make a division for the legs and taper the sides to the waist. Using tool no.12, add a row of stitch marks across the waistline and to the edge of the leg, then add a row of small vertical lines below. Shape the top from the other square as for the dress, minus the bow. Secure to the left-hand stand and add a black ball on top (**F**).

The black and white door

1 To complete the door you will need 20g (¾oz) of black sugarpaste and 10g (⅜oz) of white. Roll out all the black to a 5mm (⅛in) thickness and cut out a rectangle measuring 7 x 3cm (2¾ x 1¼in) (**G**). Glue the door to the right-hand side of the shoe shop.

2 To make the panels for the door take 5g (¼oz) of the white sugarpaste and roll out very thinly. Cut out three 1.5cm (½in) squares, attach one to the top half of the door and one to the bottom, then cut the third square in half and place this between the two larger panels (**G**). Indent the two square panels with a 1cm (⅜in) square cutter.

3 Make the canopy by rolling out the remaining 5g (¼oz) of white sugarpaste to a 3mm (⅛in) thickness. Cut out a 3.5cm (1⅜in) circle and then cut it in half. Attach to the top of the door (**G**).

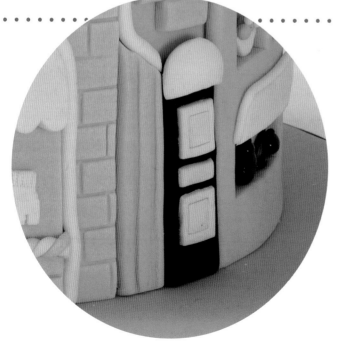

The tea shop

1 For the shop front you will need 90g (3¼oz) of pink sugarpaste rolled out to a 5mm (⅛in) thickness measuring 12 x 7cm (4¾ x 2¾in). Texture the top with the brick impression mat as before. Mark the central point at the top and make a diagonal cut on either side to slope the roof (**G**).

2 For the roof decoration roll 5g (¼oz) of white sugarpaste into a thin sausage shape 13cm (5in) long and secure to the top of the shop front. Cut out a 2cm (¾in) diamond in white and place in the centre (**G**).

3 For the windows cut out two 2cm (¾in) squares from the top of the shop front then cut out the large window opening measuring 3.5 x 5cm (1⅜ x 2in) (**G**).

4 For the window blinds roll 3g (⅛oz) of white sugarpaste into a strip measuring 1 x 6cm (⅜ x 2⅜in). Make diagonal cuts to form two blinds and attach over the top windows. For the large blind, roll out 7g (¼oz) of white sugarpaste into a strip measuring 1.5 x 6cm (½ x 2⅜in) and place over the large window (**G**). Roll a thin lace using 5g (¼oz) of white sugarpaste and attach over the top and sides of the large blind.

5 To complete all the window displays you will need 2g (⅛oz) of black sugarpaste and 1g (⅛oz) of white. To make the teapot, take a small amount of black sugarpaste, roll into a ball and flatten with your finger. Add a smaller flattened ball for the lid and a tiny ball for the knob on top. Roll the spout into an 'S' shape and glue to the side of the pot. For the handle, roll a small lace and curve it, then attach to the other side of the pot (**G**). Glue the pot inside the window at an angle.

6 For the teacup and saucer roll a small ball of black sugarpaste and flatten it. Cut off the top of the shape to make it straight. Roll the cut-off piece in your fingers again and flatten it completely to make the saucer. Roll a very tiny lace and curve it for the handle, secure to the cup and then place in the centre of the window (**G**).

7 Make the sugar bowl with lid by rolling two flattened balls of different sizes (**G**). Place the finished bowl inside the window.

8 For the white bowl roll 1g (1⁄8oz) of the white sugarpaste into a cone shape then cut off the narrow end (**G**). Secure it inside the top window and add some small balls of white and pink to the top.

9 For the black bowl roll a small ball into a short sausage shape and flatten at each end (**G**). Secure inside the top window and add some white and pink balls as before.

10 For the border at the base of the cake roll out 100g (3½oz) of pink sugarpaste to a 5mm (1⁄8in) thickness. Impress the mat over the top to reveal six rows of bricks. Cut them into three lengths, each two bricks high. Attach two strips round the back of the cake from shop to shop, interlocking the bricks at each join. With the remaining strip of two bricks high, cut out blocks of two and three bricks to decorate the remainder of the cake (**G**).

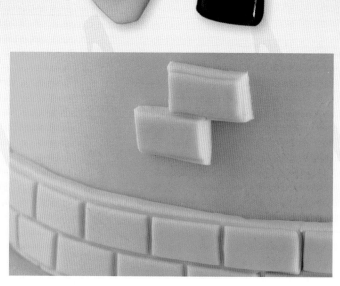

The birthday girl

1 For the body roll 44g (1½oz) of pink sugarpaste into a cone shape 7cm (2¾in) high (**H**). Place in the centre of the mini cake and push a length of dry spaghetti down through the centre and into the cake, keeping it vertical. Secure the mini cake on top of the large cake with strong edible glue.

2 For the legs roll 24g (7⁄8oz) of flesh-coloured sugarpaste into a sausage shape, making a diagonal cut in the centre. Narrow at the ankle and the back of the knee then bend each leg at the knee area. Shape the foot, which should be quite small to fit into the shoe (**H**).

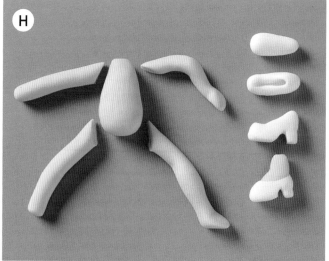

3 To make the shoes you will need 6g (¼oz) of white sugarpaste, equally divided, and then rolled into two fat cone shapes. Push the rounded end of tool no.5 into the wide end of each cone, gradually hollowing out the inside. Take your paintbrush and press the shoe over the handle to make the arch. Pull down the back to form the heel (**H**). Slip the feet into the shoes, smoothing them to fit. Add two small black balls to the front of each shoe to decorate. Attach the top of the leg to the hip and position both knees so that they are close together with the feet wide apart. Secure the backs of the legs to the cake to keep them in position.

4 For the petticoat roll 25g (⅞oz) of white sugarpaste into a strip measuring 2.5 x 22cm (1 x 8⅝in). Make gentle even folds and press along the top with your finger to prevent the frills from moving (**I**). Apply some edible glue to the tops of the legs and on the cake. Place the frill in a curved shape above the knees.

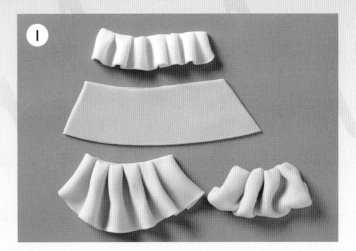

5 Make the front of the skirt by rolling 40g (1½oz) of pink sugarpaste into a strip measuring 4 x 22cm (1½ x 8⅝in). Frill as described for the petticoat (**I**) and attach around the waistline, opening out the skirt to rest on each side of the cake.

6 Make the back of the skirt by rolling 22g (¾oz) of pink sugarpaste into a strip measuring 4 x 14cm (1½ x 5½in). Frill as for the front of the skirt, but this time turn under the hem into soft folds (**I**). Apply some edible glue around the waistline at the back and arrange the skirt so that it meets the join of the front skirt.

7 For the bolero jacket you will need 18g (¾oz) of white sugarpaste. Take off 10g (⅜oz) and roll into a sausage shape, press the rolling pin into the shape and roll into a soft oval shape measuring 3.5 x 8cm (1⅜ x 3⅛in) (**J**). Apply edible glue around the back and side of the upper body and attach the bolero, bringing it round to the front. Push a short piece of dry spaghetti into the shoulders.

8 Make the sleeves using the remaining 8g (¼oz) of white sugarpaste. Equally divide, roll into two small sausage shapes and attach over the spaghetti at the shoulders (**J**). Push a further piece of dry spaghetti into the base of each sleeve to connect with the arms.

9 For the arms roll 16g (½oz) of flesh-coloured sugarpaste into a sausage shape, making a straight cut in the centre. Narrow at each wrist and elbow areas and then flatten the rounded ends with your finger to form the hands. Make a bend in each arm and make a straight cut just above the elbow (**J**). Push the left arm over the spaghetti in the sleeve and secure with edible glue. Place this arm so that the hand is cupped in an open position.

10 Attach the right arm to the sleeve, bringing the hand upwards with the palm facing outwards. To hold the arm in this position, push a piece of dry spaghetti into the palm and down through the arm and out at the elbow into the leg.

11 For the head you will need 13g (½oz) of flesh-coloured sugarpaste rolled into a ball. Pull the neck down and indent the eye area (see page 14). Make a straight cut at the neck to shorten it, and use the sugarpaste you cut off for the nose and ears. Insert the pointed end of tool no.3 to make a hole for the mouth. Roll a tiny ball of pink sugarpaste and push it inside the hole. Shape the lips by pushing tool no.3 inside the ball (**J**).

12 Draw on the eyelids, eyelashes and eyebrows using a No.0000 paintbrush and some black liquid food colour. With a dry brush, dust the eyelids with pale blue dust food colour and dust the cheeks with pale pink dust food colour (**J**). Gently slip the head over the spaghetti at the neck, turning the head slightly to the right.

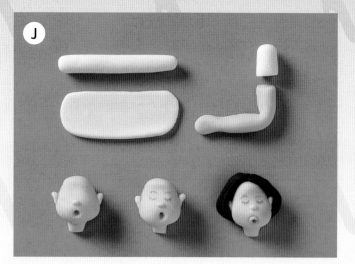

Tip
There is no need to cut the fingers into either hand, as they will be hidden.

13 For the hair soften 14g (½oz) of black sugarpaste with white vegetable fat (shortening) and fill the cup of a sugar press (or garlic press). Gently squeeze out 3cm (1¼in) lengths and glue the hair to the head a few strands at a time (**J**). Add two small round pink balls for the earrings.

14 For the white hat roll out 4g (⅛oz) of white sugarpaste and cut out a 2cm (¾in) circle for the brim. Roll the remainder into a small sausage shape and press it flat at both ends. Attach to the centre of the brim (**K**). Push a short piece of dry spaghetti into the head and slip the hat over the top, securing it to the head at a jaunty angle.

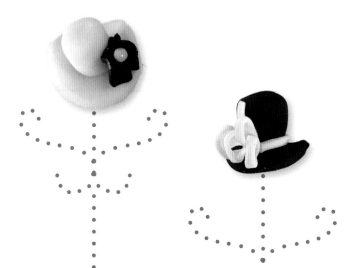

15 To make the small flower roll out 1g (⅛oz) of black sugarpaste and cut out a 1cm (⅜in) circle. Pinch the circle underneath and squeeze into the shape (**K**). Attach to the hat adding a small ball of white in the centre.

16 For the black hat you will need 5g (¼oz) of black sugarpaste. Roll out and cut a 2.5cm (1in) circle for the brim. Roll the remainder of the sugarpaste into a fat cone shape and then secure the narrow end to the centre of the brim. Roll out 2g (⅛oz) of white sugarpaste and cut into fine strips – one to go around the crown, and one cut into three to make the loops (**K**). Apply some edible glue to the palm of the right hand and place the hat on top.

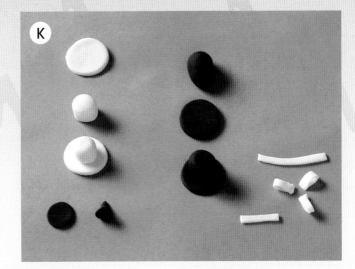

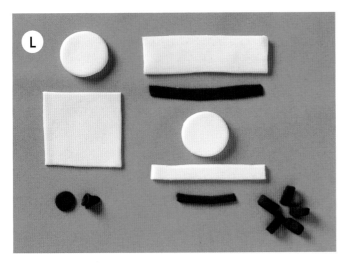

The hatbox

1 To complete the hatbox you will need 40g (1½oz) of white sugarpaste with 4g (⅛oz) of black for the trimmings. Take off 20g (¾oz) of white and roll out to a 5mm (⅛in) thickness. Cut out two 3cm (1¼in) circles, one for the base of the box and one for the lid. Roll out a strip measuring 3 x 11cm (1¼ x 4½in) for the side of the box. Apply some edible glue around the base and attach the strip, finishing with a neat seam. Set aside to dry. To make the handle for the box roll out 2g (⅛oz) of black sugarpaste and cut a piece to measure 5mm x 5cm (⅛ x 2in). Secure to each side of the box base (**L**).

2 For the lid cut out a strip in white sugarpaste measuring 1 x 11cm (⅜ x 4½in). Attach around the circle for the lid and set aside to dry. Make the decorations using the remaining black sugarpaste. Roll out a thin strip and cut into short pieces, then make five small loops. Attach the loops to the top of the lid evenly spaced out. Using the remaining black sugarpaste, cut out a 1cm (⅜in) circle and pinch in the centre to make a flower shape. Attach to the centre of the loops (**L**).

3 For the tissue paper inside the box roll out 10g (⅜oz) of the white sugarpaste thinly, cut out a 6cm (2⅜in) square (**L**) and arrange inside the box base. Attach the completed hatbox to the top of the cake with the lid resting against it.

The vanity case and shoes

1 For the case roll out 12g (½oz) of black sugarpaste to a 1cm (⅜in) thickness and cut out a 3cm (1¼in) circle (**M**). Make a straight edge at the base of the circle.

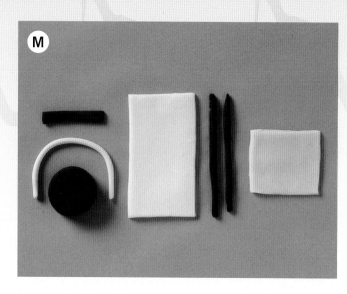

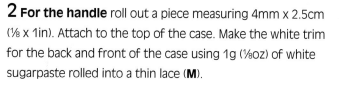

2 For the handle roll out a piece measuring 4mm x 2.5cm (⅛ x 1in). Attach to the top of the case. Make the white trim for the back and front of the case using 1g (⅛oz) of white sugarpaste rolled into a thin lace (**M**).

3 Make two shoes using 5g (¼oz) of pink sugarpaste, as described for the birthday girl's shoes (see page 79). Attach to the top of the cake with edible glue – one upright, the other on its side.

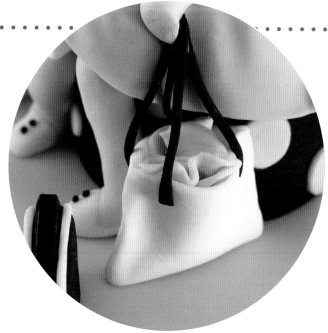

The shopping bag

1 For the bag roll out 25g (⅞oz) of white sugarpaste to measure 10 x 6cm (4 x 2⅜in) (**M**). Apply some edible glue to the side edges and fold in half, keeping the top open.

2 For the tissue paper inside the bag roll out 15g (½oz) of pink sugarpaste very thinly into a 6.5cm (2½in) square (**M**). Place inside the bag so that you can see it at the top.

3 Make the handles by rolling out 3g (⅛oz) of black sugarpaste into a lace, cut in half and attach one to either side of the bag (**M**). Secure the bag to the top of the cake directly under the hand, and secure the handles under the palm.

4 To finish the cake paint any items that you want to shine with confectioners' glaze to highlight them.

A Little More Fun!

Fashion Fancies

These stylish mini cakes with their edible hats, shoes and bags will be a guaranteed hit with the party girls. They are made using the Silverwood 6cm (2½in) round cake pans (see Suppliers, page 126 and recipe, page 22) then covered in sugarpaste and decorated with different sized spots and a twisted rope at the base. Shopping and cake ... what a great girly combination!

The Magic Crayon

Jump on board and let the magic crayon transport you to the best party in town! Boys and girls alike will enjoy the ride and you're sure to be top of the class with this creative design. You can copy this cake to the letter, or you could easily adapt the characters to depict the child whose birthday it is and his or her best school pals.

"Hold on tight, boy – this ride will knock your spots off!"

Sugarpaste

- ★ 1kg 506g (3lb 5⅛oz) orange
- ★ 1kg 175g (2lb 9½oz) white
- ★ 745g (1lb 10¼oz) yellow
- ★ 125g (4½oz) black
- ★ 121g (4½oz) green
- ★ 88g (3⅛oz) dark blue
- ★ 86g (3oz) red
- ★ 86g (3oz) flesh
- ★ 75g (2½oz) dark brown
- ★ 48g (1⅝oz) pink
- ★ 40g (1½oz) lilac
- ★ 10g (3⅛oz) light brown

Materials

- ★ 12 x 8in (30 x 20cm) cake
- ★ 3 round mini cakes, 6.5cm (2½in)
- ★ Lime paste food colour
- ★ Food colour pens in brown, green, red, blue and yellow
- ★ White edible paint
- ★ White vegetable fat (shortening)
- ★ Confectioners' glaze
- ★ Buttercream (see page 24)
- ★ Edible glue (see page 24)

Equipment

- ★ 35cm (14in) square cake drum
- ★ 30cm (12in) cake card
- ★ 9cm (3½in), 7cm (2¾in), 4cm (1½in), 2cm (¾in) and 1.5cm (½in) round cutters
- ★ 5cm (2in), 2cm (¾in) and 1cm (⅜in) square cutters
- ★ 2cm (¾in) blossom cutter
- ★ Blue ribbon 15mm (½in) wide x 160cm (63in) long
- ★ Non-toxic glue
- ★ 2 sugar presses (or garlic presses)
- ★ Flower former
- ★ Basic tool kit (see pages 10–12)

Covering the large cake and board . . . .

1 To cover the board make up some lime sugarpaste by colouring 800g (1lb 12¼oz) of white sugarpaste with lime paste food colour. Roll out the paste to an even 3mm (⅛in) thickness. Cover the board in the usual way (see page 28) trimming the edges neatly with a marzipan knife. Save 69g (2⅜oz) of the trimmings for use later. Edge the board with the blue ribbon, securing it with non-toxic glue.

2 To cover the cake you will need 1kg 500g (3lb 5oz) of orange sugarpaste. Roll out to an even 5mm (¼in) thickness and cover the cake in the usual way (see pages 26–27) – you will have 300g (10½oz) left over. Secure the cake to the board with strong edible glue (see page 24) leaving a space of 10cm (4in) at the front to allow for the decorations.

Covering the crayon cake . . . .

1 Sandwich together the three mini cakes with buttercream. Cover the whole of the cake with buttercream, and place onto a piece of greaseproof paper.

2 To complete the crayon you will need 725g (1lb 9½oz) of yellow sugarpaste. Take off 600g (1lb 5oz) and roll into a piece measuring approximately 30cm (12in) square (**A**). Place the cake on top of the sugarpaste and roll until the cake is covered. Make a neat join down the length of the cake, turning the edge of the sugarpaste over at each end and trimming the rest away. Position the join on the underside of the cake, and then place onto a cake card.

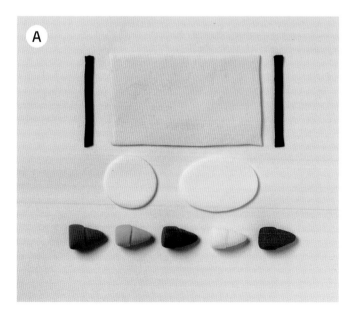

3 To seal and cover the ends of the cake cut out two 7cm (2¾in) circles in yellow sugarpaste and attach to each end. Push two pieces of dry spaghetti into the front of the crayon. Roll the remaining yellow sugarpaste into a large cone shape and slip over the spaghetti, securing with edible glue. Support the cone shape with foam until dry.

4 To make the label roll out 20g (¾oz) of white sugarpaste, cut out a 9cm (3½in) circle, then roll it out to make an oval shape. Attach this to the centre top of the crayon. Roll out 12g (½oz) of black sugarpaste and cut into two strips measuring 20 x 1cm (8 x ⅜in). Attach the strips on either side of the label (**A**).

5 Decorate the back of the crayon by making five crayon points using 7g (¼oz) each of white, lilac, red, green and blue sugarpaste. Roll each colour into a fat cone shape then push a 1.5cm (½in) round cutter over the tip to mark

a line. Trim the end flat (**A**). Push five short pieces of dry spaghetti evenly spaced around the back of the crayon and slip the crayon points over the top. Set the crayon cake aside until you are ready to add the figures.

The crayons

1 Make four jumbo crayons to stabilize the crayon cake using 27g (1oz) each of red, blue, green and lilac sugarpaste. Roll a fat cone shape 6cm (2⅜in) long in each colour. Take a 2cm (¾in) round cutter and slip it over the tip to mark a line (**B**).

2 For the labels roll out 5g (¼oz) of white sugarpaste and cut out four 1.5cm (½in) circles then roll over with your rolling pin to make them oval shapes. Attach one on each of the crayons then take 3g (⅛oz) of black sugarpaste and cut two narrow strips to place on either side (**B**). Set the four crayons aside.

3 Make three smaller crayons in the same way, using 6g (¼oz) each of orange, blue and lilac sugarpaste with 2g (⅛oz) of white for the labels and 2g (⅛oz) of black for the strips. Stack on the right-hand side of the cake board.

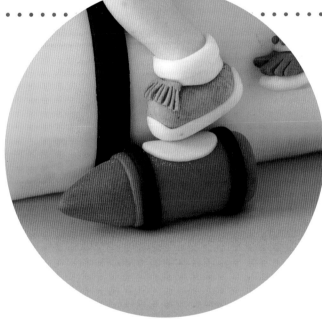

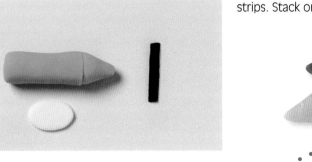
B

The Magic Crayon

The paint tubes

1 For the large paint tube take 70g (2½oz) of white sugarpaste and roll into a cone shape. Narrow the top and flatten the bottom, curling it upwards as though squeezed. Mark lines around the top with tool no.4 (**C**).

2 Make the label using 3g (⅛oz) of blue sugarpaste rolled into a strip measuring 6 x 1.5cm (2⅜ x ½in) and attach it around the tube (**C**).

3 For the lid roll 3g (⅛oz) of black sugarpaste into a ball then flatten it. Roll a further 1g (⅛oz) of black sugarpaste into a flattened ball and attach to the larger shape (**C**). Position the tube and lid on the corner of the large cake.

4 To make the blue paint roll out 40g (1½oz) of blue sugarpaste into a long sausage shape, making it bulge at the top. It should reach from the end of the tube, down the side of the cake and along the bottom (**C**).

5 Make the small paint tube in the same way using 25g (⅞oz) of white sugarpaste with 1g (⅛oz) of red for the label and 2g (⅛oz) of black for the lid. Make a round blob of paint using 5g (¼oz) of red sugarpaste and attach to the end of the tube. Secure to the left-hand corner of the cake board.

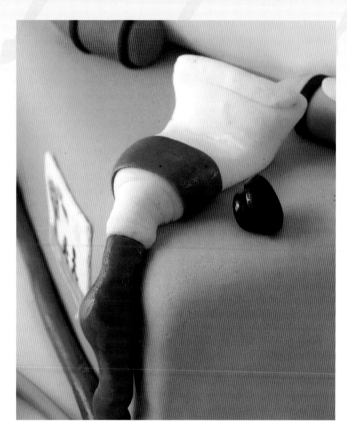

The pencil pot and pencils

1 For the pot roll 38g (1⅜oz) of green sugarpaste into a cone shape. Keeping the thicker end at the top, gently squeeze the shape to flatten it at the top and bottom. Hollow out the top with your fingers so that the pencils will sit just below the rim. Push a short piece of dry spaghetti into the centre front of the pot and add a small ball of green sugarpaste for the nose. Add two small balls of white sugarpaste for the eyes, adding two tiny black balls on the top for the pupils. Add a highlight to each eye with white edible paint on the end of a cocktail stick or toothpick. Mark a smile using the edge of a 2cm (¾in) round cutter (**D**).

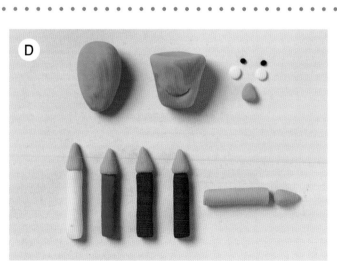

2 To make the pencils you will need 4g (⅛oz) each of red, pink, lime, yellow, dark blue and pale blue sugarpaste. To make the pale blue add 1g (⅛oz) of dark blue sugarpaste to 3g (⅛oz) of white and knead well. Roll each colour into a short sausage shape and flatten both ends (**D**). Push a piece of dry spaghetti into the top of each crayon down through the centre, leaving a little showing at the top to take the tip and at the base to push into the cup.

3 To make all the pencil tops you will need 8g (¼oz) of light brown sugarpaste. Take off a pinch for each crayon and make a small pointed cone. Flatten the base and slip over the spaghetti at the top (**D**). Arrange the crayons in the pot, making the front ones shorter. Add a black tip to the top of each pencil using a food colour pen. Attach the completed pot to the cake board with edible glue.

The books and the apple

1 To make the books you will need 14g (½oz) each of red and yellow sugarpaste for the covers and 28g (1oz) of white sugarpaste equally divided for the pages. Roll out the red sugarpaste into a rectangle measuring 4 x 8cm (1½ x 3⅛in). Take 14g (½oz) of white sugarpaste and shape it into a square with your fingers to fit into half of the book cover. Mark the pages with tool no.4, fold the cover over and mark the spine of the book with tool no.4 (**E**).

2 Repeat with the yellow sugarpaste to make the yellow book. Stack the yellow book on top of the red one and secure to the front of the cake board.

3 For the apple roll 6g (¼oz) of red sugarpaste into a smooth ball. Mark a hole at the top using tool no.3. Make the stalk by rolling the tiniest amount of dark brown sugarpaste and glue inside the hole. Take 0.5g (⅛oz) of green sugarpaste and roll into a tiny cone shape, flatten with your finger and mark the centre of the leaf, adding diagonal lines either side (**E**). Glue to the apple. Push a short piece of dry spaghetti into the top of the books and slip the apple over the top.

E

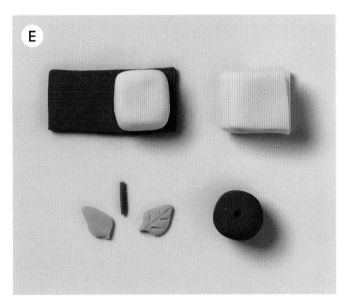

The paintbrush and paintings ·

1 For the paintbrush roll 3g (⅛oz) of green sugarpaste into a tapered sausage shape 9cm (3½in) long. Push a length of dry spaghetti into the top, leaving 1cm (⅜in) showing. Take 1g (⅛oz) of white sugarpaste and mix it with a little black sugarpaste to make a grey shade. Roll into a short sausage shape and push it over the spaghetti. Mark with tool no.4. Make the bristles with 1g (⅛oz) of light brown sugarpaste. Roll into a cone shape and attach to the top of the brush (**F**). Set aside.

2 Make the large painting by rolling out 10g (⅜oz) of white sugarpaste into a rectangle measuring 4 x 6cm (1½ x 2⅜in). Set this aside to dry before adding the picture using food colour pens (**F**). When completed attach to the front side of the large cake.

3 Make a second sheet of paper using 10g (⅜oz) of white sugarpaste measuring the same size as the large painting and cut it in half (**F**). Add the pictures with food colour pens and when dry, place these on the front of the board and attach the paintbrush on top.

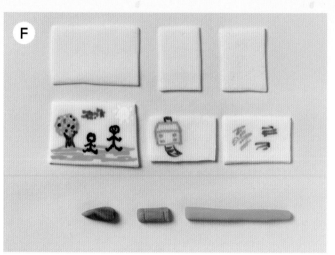

The dog

1 For the body roll 34g (1⅛oz) of white sugarpaste into a tall cone shape, curving the back (**G**). Place on the front of the crayon and insert a length of dry spaghetti down through the centre, leaving 2cm (¾in) showing at the top.

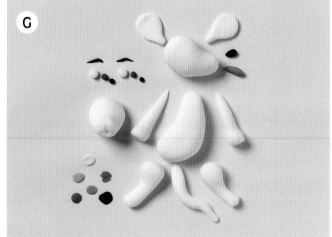

The Magic Crayon

2 For the back legs equally divide 14g (½oz) of white sugarpaste and roll into two cone shapes. Narrow each cone at the lower leg, leaving the paw rounded. Push a short piece of dry spaghetti into the hip area and slip the legs over the top. Mark the paws using tool no.4 (**G**).

3 For the front legs roll 8g (¼oz) of white sugarpaste into a sausage shape, cutting the sausage in half. Turn up the rounded ends to form the paws. Turn the legs over on to their side and using tool no.4, remove the bulk from the back of the leg by making a diagonal cut. Attach the legs to the front of the body (**G**).

4 Make the tail using the white left over from the legs. Roll a tapered cone shape and make a diagonal cut at the thickest end. Attach this to the back of the dog (**G**).

5 For the head roll 17g (½oz) of white sugarpaste into a cone shape. Flatten the cone shape at the front, giving you room to mark the features at the front. Using tool no.4, mark a line down the centre and mark a diagonal line on either side to form the mouth. Insert tool no.5 to open

the mouth. Take 0.5g (⅛oz) of pink sugarpaste, roll into a cone shape for the tongue and insert inside the hole. Add a small black cone shape for nose (**G**).

6 To make the ears equally divide 1g (⅛oz) of white sugarpaste and roll into two cone shapes, then flatten with your finger. Attach to each side of the head securing into place using tool no.1 (**G**).

7 For the eyes make two small round balls in white, then add two small brown balls and finally two tiny black balls for the pupils with a dot of white edible paint. Roll two very thin banana shapes to outline the eyes. Slip the head over the spaghetti at the neck and turn to look left. Finally add spots using a variety of colours (**G**).

The girl in pink . . . .

1 For the body take 43g (1½oz) of the lime sugarpaste left over from covering the board and roll into a cone shape (**H**). Attach the cone to the top of the crayon cake behind the dog, then push a length of dry spaghetti down through the centre, leaving 2cm (¾in) showing at the top. Push a short piece of dry spaghetti into the hip area on either side of the body.

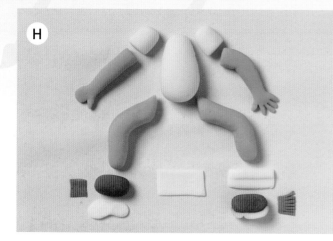

2 Make the legs using 32g (1oz) of flesh-coloured sugarpaste rolled into a sausage shape 15cm (6in) long. Make a diagonal cut in the centre, bending each leg at the knee. Attach the legs over the spaghetti at the hips, keeping the knees in a bent position (**H**). Push a short piece of dry spaghetti into the bottom of each leg leaving 1cm (⅜in) showing to support the shoes.

3 For the shoes equally divide 8g (¼oz) of pink sugarpaste and roll into two oval shapes. Make the soles using 2g (⅛oz) of white sugarpaste equally divided, shape into two oval shapes and flatten. Attach to the base of each shoe, bringing the sole up at the front and back. Mark the heels with tool no.4. Slip the shoes over the spaghetti at the legs. Cut two 1cm (⅜in) pink squares and mark with a fringe using tool no.4. Attach to the front of each shoe (**H**).

4 Make the socks using 1g (⅛oz) of white sugarpaste rolled out thinly into a rectangle. Make two. Turn the tops over, and attach around each ankle (**H**).

5 For the sleeves equally divide 12g (½oz) of the leftover lime sugarpaste and roll into two small sausage shapes (**H**). Slip the sleeves over the spaghetti at the top of the body, then push a small piece of dry spaghetti into the end of each sleeve to secure the arms.

6 To make the arms roll 14g (½oz) of flesh-coloured sugarpaste into a sausage shape. Cut the sausage shape in half and then press down the rounded ends to form the hands. Make the hands as described on page 16. Narrow each arm at the wrist and bend at the elbow (**H**). Make a straight cut just above each elbow and attach to the spaghetti at the base of each sleeve.

7 For the petticoat roll out 12g (½oz) of white sugarpaste and cut out a 4cm (1½in) circle. Using either the end of your paintbrush or a frilling tool, place on the edge of the circle, move the tool backwards and forwards pressing lightly to make the frill (see page 18). Take a 2cm (¾in) circle out of the centre (**I**) and slip over the body.

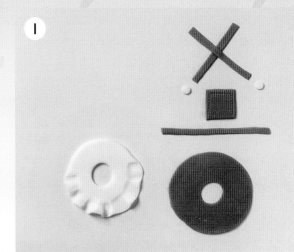

Tip
When making the frill, keep the
pressure light – if you press too
hard it will only make a ridge.

8 For the dress roll out 25g (⅞oz) of pink sugarpaste and cut out a 7cm (2¾in) circle, but this time do not frill the edges. Take out the centre with a 2cm (¾in) round cutter and slip this over the petticoat. Cut out a 2cm (¾in) square using 2g (⅛oz) of pink sugarpaste. Stitch mark three sides using tool no.12 (**I**) and attach to the centre of the body.

9 For the waistband and straps roll a thin strip from 2g (⅛oz) of pink sugarpaste. Attach around the join at the waist. Cut out two thin strips from another 2g (⅛oz) of pink sugarpaste for the straps and set aside, keeping them covered to prevent them drying out. Attach the girl's left hand to the top of the dress and the right hand to the dog. Attach the straps to the dress and cross them over at the back. Add two small lime buttons to the front (**I**).

10 For the head roll 20g (¾oz) of flesh-coloured sugarpaste into a ball. Pull down the neck at the base of the ball by twisting it gently between your thumb and finger. Indent the eye area (see page 14) and make a straight cut at the base of the neck (**J**). Use the sugarpaste you have cut off to make the nose and ears. Place the head inside a flower former to keep the shape.

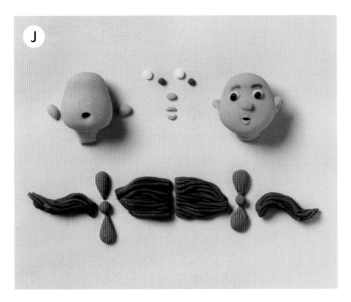

11 For the nose roll a tiny oval shape and secure to the centre of the face. Using tool no.11, mark a smile. Open the mouth wider using the soft end of your paintbrush. Add two small banana shapes for the lips (**J**).

12 For the eyes roll two small white balls and place them just above and on either side of the nose. Add two tiny round balls of blue sugarpaste for the irises, pressing them on lightly with your finger (**J**).

13 For the ears roll two small cone shapes and attach to each side of the head, keeping the tops level with the centre of the eyes. Indent the base of each ear with the end of your paintbrush (**J**).

14 For the hair soften 20g (¾oz) of dark brown sugarpaste with white vegetable fat (shortening) and fill the sugar press (or garlic press). Mark a line for the parting down the centre of the head. Cover the head with edible glue then extrude strands of hair, placing them from the parting outwards so the head is covered in two sections (**J**).

15 Make the bunches by extruding longer strands of hair and arranging them into a bunch (**J**). Attach them at the side of the head. Make some soft wisps of hair for the front by rolling a little dark brown sugarpaste into very fine elongated cone shapes.

16 Add two bows using 1g (⅛oz) of pink sugarpaste. Roll two small flattened cones and then place at the top of the bunches, with the points of each meeting in the centre, then add a small ball in the middle of each to complete (**J**).

The girl in green ....

1 For the body roll 43g (1½oz) of white sugarpaste into a cone shape (**K**). Attach the cone to centre of the crayon cake, behind the girl in pink. Push a length of dry spaghetti down through the centre of the cone, leaving 2cm (¾in) showing at the top. Push a short piece of dry spaghetti into the hip area on both sides of the body.

2 For the legs roll 20g (¾oz) of dark brown sugarpaste into a sausage shape 15cm (6in) long. Make a diagonal cut in the centre, bending each leg at the knee. Turn the rounded ends upwards to form the feet. Make the feet as described on page 16. Mark the nails with the end of a piece of dry spaghetti (**K**). Attach the legs over the spaghetti at the hips.

3 For the flip-flops equally divide 4g (⅛oz) of white sugarpaste. Roll into two small sausage shapes and flatten with your finger, marking the undersides with tool no.4 to make the heels. Attach to the bottom of each foot. Roll out 1g (⅛oz) of green sugarpaste and cut a thin strip to go around the top of each foot, and then decorate each shoe with three tiny balls of pink sugarpaste (**L**).

4 To make the skirt roll out 25g (⅞oz) of white sugarpaste and cut out a 7cm (2¾in) circle, then take out the centre using a 2cm (¾in) round cutter. Make the flower decorations by rolling out 10g (⅜oz) of green sugarpaste and cutting out six 2cm (¾in) blossoms. Set one blossom

aside for the collar. Apply a little edible glue to the back of each blossom and space out around the skirt. Lightly roll over them to integrate them into the white sugarpaste (**L**). Slip the skirt over the body, arranging it carefully over the top of the legs.

5 For the T-shirt roll out 27g (1oz) of green sugarpaste and cut out two 5cm (2in) squares, then make a diagonal cut at the shoulder seams (**L**). Apply a little edible glue around the body and place one square to the back. The side seams should run in a horizontal line down each side – if they don't, use tool no.4 to take off any excess. Trim off at the neck if necessary. Place the second square at the front and trim the sides as before to make a perfect join on both sides. Push a piece of dry spaghetti into each shoulder.

6 For the sleeves roll 8g (¼oz) of green sugarpaste into two balls (**L**). Attach these over the spaghetti at the shoulders, then push another short piece of spaghetti into the base of each sleeve to support the arms.

7 To make the arms you will need 14g (½oz) of dark brown sugarpaste. Follow the instructions for making as for the girl in pink (see page 92) (**L**). Rest the right palm on the knee and the left arm on the skirt.

8 For the collar roll out 10g (⅜oz) of white sugarpaste and cut out a 5cm (2in) circle. Make the circle into a horseshoe shape by taking out another 3cm (1¼in) circle. Attach the green blossom you made earlier to the back of the collar and secure around the neck, bringing the points to the front. Make a 2cm (¾in) blossom using 1g (⅛oz) of white sugarpaste and attach to the front of the T-shirt, adding a small ball of pink sugarpaste to the centre (**L**).

9 For the head roll 20g (¾oz) of dark brown sugarpaste into a ball and then pull down the neck. Indent the eye area (see page 14) (**K**). Make a straight cut at the base of the neck and use the paste you cut off to make the nose, eyes and ears. Place the head into a flower former.

10 For the nose roll a small oval shape of dark brown sugarpaste and attach to the centre of the face (**K**).

11 Make the eyes using two small balls of white sugarpaste, two smaller dark brown balls for the irises and two even smaller black balls on top for the pupils. Make two small cone shapes for the ears and secure to the side of the head, indenting them with the end of your paintbrush (**K**).

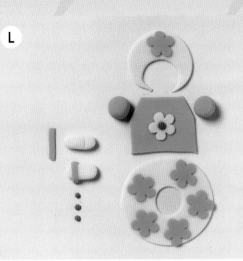

L

12 Mark a smile using tool no.11 and open the mouth using the soft end of your paintbrush. Make a tiny banana shape in white for the teeth and attach inside the smile. For the lips roll two small banana shapes in brown with a pinch of pink added (**K**). Attach the head over the spaghetti at the neck, turning it to look behind her.

13 To make the hair you will need two sugar presses (or garlic presses). Soften 20g (¾oz) of black sugarpaste and 2g (⅛oz) of white sugarpaste with white vegetable fat (shortening). Take one sugar press and smooth a thin layer of the white sugarpaste into the holes. Next fill the cup half full with the black sugarpaste and squeeze out short strands of hair. Arrange all around the head into the required style. When you have emptied the first sugar press once, use the second press to finish making the hair (**K**).

The boy

1 Make the body and legs in one piece by rolling 58g (2oz) of black sugarpaste into a carrot shape. Turn the shape around so that the thickest part is at the bottom. Smooth and flatten the shape, then using a sharp knife, divide the shape in half forming two legs. Soften and round off the edges with your fingers (**M**). Hollow out the ends of the trousers using tool no.3. Push a piece of dry spaghetti into each trouser leg to support the lower legs and into each shoulder to support the arms. Position the body in a sitting position on the end of the crayon and push a piece of dry spaghetti down through the centre, leaving 2cm (¾in) showing at the top.

2 To make the lower legs with feet equally divide 8g (¼oz) of white sugarpaste and roll into two sausage shapes. Turn up the feet at one end of each sausage and mark the toes with tool no.4 (**M**). Push the legs over the spaghetti in the the the trousers.

3 For the flip-flops equally divide 4g (⅛oz) of black sugarpaste. Roll into two small sausage shapes and flatten. Mark the heels with tool no.4. Attach to the feet and roll two thin laces for the straps (**M**).

4 Make up 30g (1oz) of a pale flesh colour by mixing 20g (¾oz) of flesh-coloured sugarpaste with 10g (⅜oz) of white. Take off 10g (⅜oz) to make the arms and roll into a sausage shape. Make a straight cut in the centre. Flatten the rounded ends to form the hands then make the fingers as described on page 16 (**M**). Push the arms over the spaghetti at the shoulders.

5 Make the tunic in one piece, including the sleeves. Roll out 22g (¾oz) of red sugarpaste into a rectangle measuring 8 x 6cm (3⅛ x 2⅜ in) (**M**). Place the centre of this piece over the spaghetti at the neck and pinch it underneath the arms to form the sleeves. Fold the sides together and trim a little if necessary then position the arms as required.

6 For the head roll 20g (¾oz) of the pale flesh sugarpaste into a ball and pull down the neck. Keep the face in a round shape and add a small ball for the nose. Mark the mouth with tool no.11 then open it up with the soft end of your paintbrush. Add two small banana shapes for the lips (**M**).

7 Make the eyes by rolling two tiny teardrop shapes in white and place them on a slant just above and on either side of the nose. Add two small black balls for the pupils. Using pale flesh sugarpaste, make two very small eyelids by rolling a short round lace and attach over each eye. Outline the bottom of each eye with a black food colour pen. Add fine eyebrows using a tiny amount of light brown sugarpaste rolled into a short lace (**M**).

8 For the ears add two small cone shapes in pale flesh sugarpaste and secure to either side of the head (**M**). Place the head over the spaghetti at the neck and turn it to look at the girl in green.

Tip
Food colour pens work better when the sugarpaste has dried.

9 For the hair fill a sugar press (or garlic press) with 10g (⅜oz) of black sugarpaste softened with white vegetable fat (shortening). Apply a thin layer all around the head (**M**).

10 Make the tunic trimming using 2g (⅛oz) of black sugarpaste rolled out into a thin strip. Attach around the edge of the sleeves and to the front of the tunic. Make the collar by rolling 1g (⅛oz) of black sugarpaste into a strip measuring 5mm x 6cm (⅛ x 2⅜in) and attach around the neck, shaping the end into a point with tool no.4 (**M**).

11 With all the figures in place, attach the crayon cake diagonally across the large cake and secure with strong edible glue. Attach two jumbo crayons on each side to help stabilize the large crayon. Apply confectioners' glaze to the blue and red paint splodges and paint tube lids to make them shine.

A Little More Fun!

Creative Cupcakes

The colourful crayon cases on these cupcakes make them the perfect partners for the main cake. Simply bake some cupcakes using the recipe on page 22, cover the tops with a circle of rolled out sugarpaste then add motifs such as crayons, paint tubes or books. These little cakes would be great on their own for a 'back to school' gathering – why not make some for your child to take in on their first day back?

Girls' Night In

Her hair is looking great and the pedicure is a real treat — this birthday girl is being well and truly pampered by her favourite friends. This fun cake is definitely a man-free zone and is perfect for any woman's birthday when a relaxing and indulgent night in with the girls is the order of the day.

"I'm glad we stayed in, girlfriend, 'cause these tunes are hot!"

You will need

Sugarpaste

* ✹ 2kg 410g (5lb 5oz) white
* ✹ 305g (10¾oz) dark brown (chocolate flavoured)
* ✹ 140g (5oz) black
* ✹ 135g (4¾oz) blue
* ✹ 106g (3¾oz) yellow
* ✹ 71g (2½oz) orange
* ✹ 47g (1⅝oz) light brown
* ✹ 34g (1⅛oz) pale blue
* ✹ 3g (⅛oz) red
* ✹ 2g (⅛oz) pink

Materials

* ✹ 25cm (10in) hexagonal cake
* ✹ Paste food colour in rose, plum and lime
* ✹ Rainbow Dust edible glitter in sparkle pink and sky blue
* ✹ Rainbow Dust sparkle stars
* ✹ White edible paint
* ✹ White vegetable fat (shortening)
* ✹ Confectioners' glaze
* ✹ Edible glue (see page 24)

Equipment

* ✹ 32cm (13in) hexagonal cake drum
* ✹ 30cm (12in), 15cm (6in) and 10cm (4in) cake cards
* ✹ 2cm (¾in) blossom cutter
* ✹ 3cm (1¼in), 2cm (¾in) and 1cm (⅜in) round cutters
* ✹ 1.5cm (½in) and 1cm (⅜in) square cutters
* ✹ Wood-textured rolling pin
* ✹ Pink ribbon 15mm (½in) wide x 120cm (47in) long
* ✹ Non-toxic glue
* ✹ Sugar press (or garlic press)
* ✹ Flower former
* ✹ Basic tool kit (see pages 10–12)

Covering the cake . . . .

1 To cover the cake you will need 1kg 200g (2lb 10¼oz) of white sugarpaste coloured with rose paste food colour. Knead the paste colour into the sugarpaste well until you have the depth of colour you require.

2 Roll out the sugarpaste to an even 5mm (⅛in) thickness. Prepare the cake as desired and cover in the usual way (see pages 26–27), making sure the edges are trimmed neatly. Set the cake aside onto a 30cm (12in) cake card. Save the remaining sugarpaste for the decorations on the board.

Covering and decorating the board . . . .

1 To cover the board you will need 600g (1lb 5oz) of white sugarpaste coloured with plum paste food colour. Knead in the colour well until you have a deep shade.

2 Moisten the edges of the board with cooled boiled water. Roll out the sugarpaste to an even 3mm (⅛in) thickness and cut out six strips measuring 5 x 24cm (2 x 9½in). Work with one strip at a time and keep the others covered to prevent them drying out. Place one strip neatly along the edge of the first section of the board, allowing any excess length to overhang at either end.

3 Place the second strip along the edge of the next section, keeping the outside edge very straight, and allow this strip to overlap the end of the first strip. Using a marzipan knife, place the blade at the pointed edge of the board and cut through both thicknesses. Remove the excess paste from the top and the bottom layers to leave a perfect join. Continue to move around the board in sections until you have covered it all.

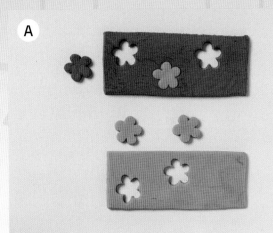

4 Using a 2cm (¾in) blossom cutter, take some shapes out of the sugarpaste around the board (**A**).

5 Roll out the leftover rose sugarpaste to an even 3mm (⅛in) thickness. Cut out some blossom shapes using the 2cm (¾in) cutter and place them inside the empty shapes on the board. Smooth over the top so that the surface is level (**A**).

6 When the decoration is complete, attach the cake to the centre of the board then sprinkle the board with Rainbow Dust sparkle stars. Edge the board with the pink ribbon, securing it with non-toxic glue.

The chair and the stool

1 Mix together 366g (13oz) of white sugarpaste with 20g (¾oz) of black to make a grey shade. Take off 240g (8½oz) and shape the base of the chair into a 6cm (2⅜in) square. Using a wood-textured rolling pin, press the design onto the side and top of the seat (**B**). Set the base aside onto a 10cm (4in) cake card.

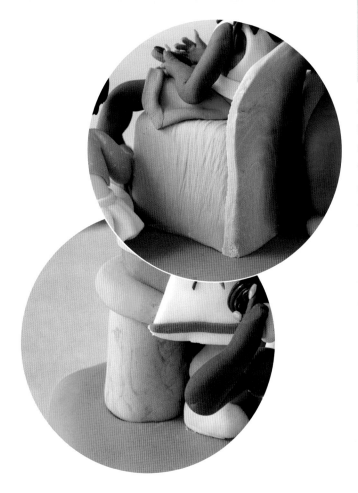

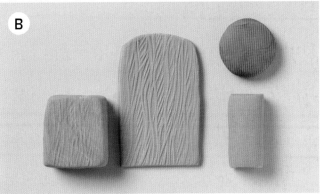

2 Make the back of the chair using 80g (2⅞oz) of grey sugarpaste. Roll out to an even 5mm (⅛in) thickness and cut out a rectangle measuring 10 x 7cm (4 x 2¾in). Run the textured rolling pin over the top and then round off one end of the shape (**B**). Place the rounded end over the top of a small rolling pin to curve it slightly. Set aside to dry then attach to the back of the seat.

3 For the stool roll the remaining 66g (2¼oz) of grey sugarpaste into a thick sausage shape. Trim to a height of 5cm (2in) (**B**) and set the leftover grey sugarpaste aside. Push a piece of dry spaghetti down through the centre, leaving 5mm (⅛in) showing at the top.

4 To make the top of the stool mix 42g (1½oz) of white sugarpaste with some rose paste food colour and roll into a ball. Flatten the ball with the palm of your hand to shape into a rounded cushion (**B**). Attach to the top of the stool and set aside to dry.

The girl on the chair . . . .

1 To make the body roll 53g (1⅞oz) of dark brown sugarpaste into a cone shape then pinch out the neck area (**C**). Flatten the cone slightly and place it on the top of the chair, leaving some room between the chair and body in order to dress her. Push a length of dry spaghetti down through the centre, leaving 1cm (⅜in) showing at the neck. Push a short piece of spaghetti into the shoulder area.

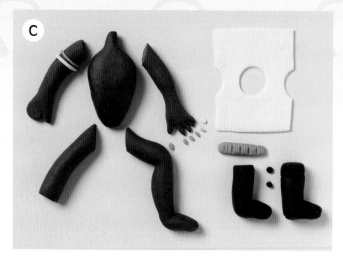

2 For the top roll out 18g (¾oz) of yellow sugarpaste and cut out a rectangle measuring 11 x 5cm (4½ x 2in). Make the neckline by taking out a 2cm (¾in) circle in the centre then, using the same cutter, take out a little sugarpaste at the shoulders (**C**). Apply edible glue to the body and slip the top over the neck. Close the side seam to neaten.

3 For the boots equally divide 22g (¾oz) of black sugarpaste and roll into two sausage shapes. Turn up one end of each to form the feet, and using tool no.4, mark around the side of each to form the soles. Mark a line 5mm (⅛in) from the top using tool no.4. Add two small buttons to the side of each boot to decorate (**C**). Set aside.

4 For the right leg roll 15g (½oz) of dark brown sugarpaste into a sausage shape 9cm (3½in) long. Make a diagonal cut at the top and a straight cut at the bottom (**C**), push a piece of dry spaghetti into this end to support the boot. Bend the leg at the knee and slip the boot over the spaghetti. Attach the leg to the body, with the back of the knee over the edge of the chair and the foot on the floor.

5 Make a cuff using 1g (⅛oz) of pink sugarpaste, rolled into a sausage shape 4cm (1½in) long. Press lightly to flatten and use tool no.12 to stitch mark vertical lines to decorate (**C**). Attach over the join between the boot and the leg.

6 For the left leg roll 20g (¾oz) of dark brown sugarpaste into a sausage shape. Indent the back of the knee and ankle, then turn up the rounded end to form the foot. Using tool no.4, mark out the big toe then round off the edges. Move the big toe away from the rest of the foot and divide the remainder into four toes, rounding them off once again. Bend the leg at the knee area (**C**) and carefully set this leg aside, keeping it covered to prevent it drying out.

7 Make a sausage shape from 20g (¾oz) of dark brown sugarpaste the same thickness as the right leg, bend it at the knee area and position it in the place of the left leg, but do not add any glue (this is just a dummy and will be removed when the left leg is attached later).

8 To complete the skirt you will need 30g (1oz) of blue sugarpaste. To make the back of the skirt, take off 9g (⅜oz) and roll into a banana shape. Place this behind the body, bringing the points to the side. Roll out the remaining blue sugarpaste into a shape for the skirt measuring 5 x 13cm (2 x 5in) (**D**). Roll the shape into a curve, and then turn under the side edges. Attach neatly around the waistline and let the skirt fall over the sides of the chair.

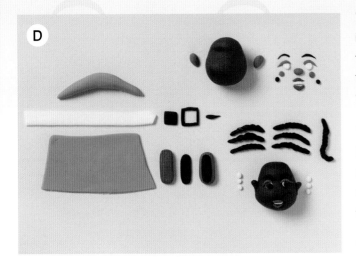

9 For the belt roll out 1g (⅛oz) of white sugarpaste and cut out a strip measuring 1 x 13cm (⅜ x 5in). Attach around the waist, allowing the end of the strip to hang over the front. Make a large buckle for the front by rolling out 1g (⅛oz) of black sugarpaste thinly and cutting a 1.5cm (½in) square. Take out the centre with a 1cm (⅜in) square cutter. Attach to the front of the belt and roll a tiny lace to place on the top (**D**).

10 For the arms roll 30g (1oz) of dark brown sugarpaste into a sausage shape. Make a diagonal cut in the centre and flatten the rounded ends with your finger slightly. Make the hands as described on page 16. Narrow the arms at the wrists and bend at the elbows (**C**).

11 Make some fingernails using some pink sugarpaste left over from covering the cake. Roll tiny oval shapes and attach to each finger with edible glue (**C**). Attach each arm over the spaghetti at the shoulders, bringing the hands forwards on the knees.

12 Make two bangles for the right arm using leftover sugarpaste from the top and skirt. Roll a thin lace in each colour and attach around the arm. Roll a small yellow oval shape for the ring and attach with edible glue to the right hand (**C**).

13 For the head roll 15g (½oz) of dark brown sugarpaste into a ball. Indent the eye area (see page 14) and place the head into a flower former. Roll a small oval shape for the nose and place this in the centre of the face. Using tool no.11, mark the mouth with a smile. Using the soft end of your paintbrush, open the lips and make the top line straight. Take a tiny amount of white sugarpaste and roll into a banana shape for the teeth. Glue the teeth into position then mark them with tool no.4. Lighten some dark brown sugarpaste with some pink sugarpaste to make the lips. Roll two small banana shapes and attach above and below the teeth (**D**).

Tip
Model the girl on the chair on a cake card, then position on top of the cake when completed, minus the left leg.

14 To make the eyes roll two tiny balls of white sugarpaste and attach them just above and on either side of the nose. Roll two smaller balls of dark brown sugarpaste and place on top of the white. Finally add tiny black pupils on the top. Outline the bottom of the eye with a very thin lace of black sugarpaste. To make the eyelids, roll two banana shapes of dark brown sugarpaste and attach over the top of each eye. Roll two thin tapered shapes for the eyebrows in black sugarpaste and attach over the eyes (**D**). Using a dry brush, apply some Rainbow Dust sparkle pink edible glitter to each eyelid.

15 For the ears roll two cone shapes in dark brown sugarpaste, attach to the side of the face and indent with the end of your paintbrush. Slip the head over the spaghetti at the neck. Using 0.5g (⅛oz) of yellow sugarpaste, roll six small balls with two slightly larger than the others. Glue three together with the larger one at the bottom to make each earring and attach to each ear (**D**).

16 For the hair soften 35g (1¼oz) of black sugarpaste with white vegetable fat (shortening) and fill the cup of a sugar press (or garlic press). Extrude the hair and take three stands at a time, twisting them to make the locks (**D**). Apply edible glue all over the head and then layer the hair from the centre parting outwards until you have covered the head. Allow some long hair to hang over the shoulders and the back of the chair.

17 For the mobile (cell) phone take 1g (⅛oz) of red sugarpaste and roll into a small sausage shape. Press down lightly to flatten with your finger, then roll 0.5g (⅛oz) of black sugarpaste into a sausage shape and flatten to fit on top of the phone (**D**). Secure to the girl's hand with edible glue.

18 Now that you have completed the girl on the chair (minus her left leg, which will be added later), place her in the centre of the cake and secure with edible glue.

The girl applying the nail polish

1 For the shoes equally divide 8g (¼oz) of orange sugarpaste and 4g (⅛oz) of white. Roll the orange sugarpaste into a small sausage shape to make the shoe, and then take half of the white sugarpaste and roll into a sausage shape to make the sole. Flatten slightly with your finger and attach to the base of the shoe. Using tool no.4, mark a line across the sole to define the heel. Take off a small amount of the remaining white sugarpaste, roll into a ball and flatten to make the circle at the front of the shoe (**E**). Make two.

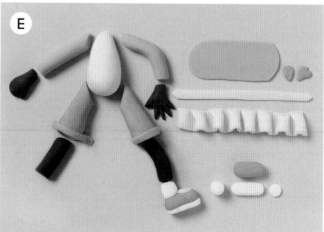

E

2 For the socks use the remaining white sugarpaste rolled into two sausage shapes (**E**). Attach one to the top of each shoe and then insert a length of dry spaghetti through the centre of the sock top, leaving 2cm (¾in) showing at the top. Set the shoes aside.

3 For the body roll 53g (1⅞oz) of yellow sugarpaste into a cone shape and place onto a 15cm (6in) cake card (**E**). Push a piece of dry spaghetti down through the body, leaving 2cm (¾in) showing at the top.

Tip
Give the cone shape for the body height so that you have room to dress the upper body.

4 For the shorts equally divide 32g (1oz) of orange sugarpaste. Roll into two sausage shapes and make a diagonal cut at the top of each. Using the pointed end of tool no.3, hollow out the other ends ready to insert the lower legs. Make turn-ups by rolling out 1g (⅛oz) of orange sugarpaste into a strip measuring 5mm x 10cm (⅛ x 4in). Divide in half and attach around the edge of the shorts (**E**).

5 For the lower legs roll 14g (½oz) of dark brown sugarpaste into a sausage shape 10cm (4in) long and cut in half. Bend each leg at the knee and then push a short piece of dry spaghetti into the top of each leg. Apply some edible glue to the tops and insert the legs into the ends of the shorts. Attach the shoes and socks to the legs (**E**) then secure to the body, crossing one leg over the other.

6 For the skirt roll out 30g (1oz) of yellow sugarpaste into a strip measuring 2 x 29cm (¾ x 11½in). Frill the strip by holding one end in your left hand, passing it from your right hand into your left hand and folding it as you go, making sure you do not crease the folds. Make the top edge of the frill straight and attach around the body (**E**).

7 For the belt roll 4g (⅛oz) of yellow sugarpaste into a length measuring 5mm x 16cm (⅛ x 6¼in). Attach the belt around the top of the frill, crossing it over on the left side. Make two small hearts by equally dividing 0.5g (⅛oz) of

orange sugarpaste and rolling into two tiny cone shapes. Mark the top of each cone with a line in the centre using tool no.4 and flatten to shape (**E**). Attach one to the belt and one to the centre of the chest.

8 For the jacket roll 8g (¼oz) of pale blue sugarpaste into a sausage shape and roll over with a rolling pin to make a strip with rounded ends (**E**). Apply some edible glue around the back and side of the body and attach the jacket. Push a short piece of dry spaghetti into the shoulders.

9 To make the arms roll 26g (1oz) of pale blue sugarpaste into a sausage shape 6cm (2⅜in) long. Make a diagonal cut in the centre and bend at the elbows (**E**). Slip the top of each arm over the spaghetti at the shoulders and bring the elbows onto the knees. Push a short piece of dry spaghetti into each wrist. Add some spots to the jacket using some white edible paint and a no.0000 paintbrush.

10 To make the hands equally divide 4g (⅛oz) of dark brown sugarpaste. Roll into two cone shapes and flatten. Make the fingers as described on page 16, then slip the hands over the spaghetti at the wrists. Turn the middle fingers on the left hand towards the palm – the index finger and thumb will hold the brush, so leave them in an open position. Place the girl on the top of the cake in front of the chair.

11 Remove the sausage from under the skirt of the girl on the chair. Secure her left leg under the skirt and rest the foot on the knee of the sitting girl. Apply some edible glue to her right palm and attach to the back of the leg. Add one pink nail to the big toe.

12 **To make the head** roll 25g (⅞oz) of dark brown sugarpaste into a ball. Pull down the neck and roll it in between your finger and thumb. Indent the eye area (see page 14) and make a straight cut at the base of the neck. Using the paste you cut off, roll two small cone shapes for the ears (**F**). Make the remainder as described for the girl on the chair (see pages 103–104), excluding the eyelids. Slip the head over the spaghetti at the neck.

13 **For the hair** soften 20g (¾oz) of black sugarpaste with white vegetable fat (shortening) and fill the cup of the sugar press (or garlic press). Extrude the hair, taking off several strands at a time. Make a straight cut at the bottom of the hair, then turn it under. Apply the hair around the back and sides of the head. Repeat for the front, placing the edge with the straight cut onto the hairline, and then fold the hair over towards the back of the head (**F**).

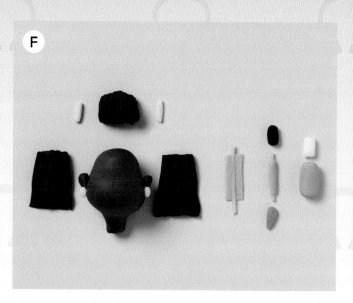

14 **For the hair slides and earrings** equally divide 0.5g (⅛oz) of yellow sugarpaste and roll into two short sausage shapes. Attach one on either side of the roll at the front of the head. Roll two small balls of yellow sugarpaste and attach one to each ear (**F**).

The nail polish and brush

1 **Make the bottle of nail polish** using 1g (⅛oz) of pink sugarpaste rolled into a sausage shape. Flatten the top and bottom of the shape. Roll 0.5g (⅛oz) of white sugarpaste into a smaller sausage shape for the neck of the bottle and attach to the top (**F**). Secure the bottle to the side of the girl.

2 **Make the brush handle** using 0.5g (⅛oz) of grey sugarpaste, rolled out thinly to measure 1cm x 5mm (⅜ x ⅛in). Run a line of edible glue down the centre of the strip and place a short piece of dry spaghetti over the top. Fold the sugarpaste over the spaghetti and cut off the excess with tool no.4. Roll the piece on the work surface to narrow it and expose the spaghetti at both ends. To make the grip, roll 0.5g (⅛oz) of black sugarpaste into a short sausage shape and push over the spaghetti at one end (**F**).

3 **For the brush head** roll a cone shape of pink sugarpaste and attach to the other end of the handle over the spaghetti (**F**). Apply some edible glue to the girl's left hand and place the brush between her finger and thumb.

The girl with the headphones ·········

1 **First make the white cushion** for her to rest against. Shape 78g (2¾oz) of white sugarpaste into a rectangle measuring 7 x 5cm (2¾ x 2in). Prop it up against the side of the chair.

2 **For the body** colour 79g (2¾oz) of white sugarpaste with lime paste food colour. Take off 56g (2oz) and roll into a cone shape for the body (**G**). Place the cone in front of the cushion and push a piece of dry spaghetti down through the centre, leaving 2cm (¾in) showing at the top. Rest the cone shape on the cushion.

3 **For the legs** roll 18g (¾oz) of white sugarpaste into a sausage shape. Divide with a diagonal cut in the centre and bend the legs at the knee area. Using the pointed end of tool no.3, hollow out the ends of the legs (**G**).

4 **For the feet** equally divide 14g (½oz) of dark brown sugarpaste and roll into two sausage shapes. Turn up at one end of each to form the feet. Mark out the big toes and divide the remainder of each foot into four toes. Roll the edges smooth and mark the toenails with a piece of dry spaghetti. Make a straight edge at the top of each shape and push a piece of dry spaghetti into the top. Apply some edible glue and push the feet into the base of the trouser legs (**G**). Attach each leg to the body and, keeping the legs bent, cross one leg over the other. Support under the knees with a piece of foam until dry.

5 **For the skirt** roll out 13g (½oz) of the lime sugarpaste into a strip measuring 2 x 23cm (¾ x 9in). Frill as described for the girl applying the nail polish (see page 105) and attach neatly around the waist (**G**). Set the remaining 10g (⅜oz) of lime sugarpaste aside.

6 **Make the bolero jacket** using 12g (½oz) of white sugarpaste coloured with plum paste food colour. Take off 4g (⅛oz) and roll out, then cut out two 3cm (1¼in) circles. Attach one circle on each side of the body and push a short piece of dry spaghetti into the shoulder. To make the sleeves, equally divide 8g (¼oz) of the plum sugarpaste and roll into two balls. Slip the balls over the spaghetti at the shoulders (**G**).

G

7 **To make the arms** roll 14g (½oz) of dark brown sugarpaste into a sausage shape 12cm (4¾in) long. Cut the sausage in half and form the hands at the rounded ends. Flatten slightly with your finger then cut out the thumbs and the index fingers only, rounding off the edges until smooth. Place the tip of tool no.4 on the work surface and indent the other three fingers of each hand, not cutting them out. Bend each arm at the elbow and cut off some of the upper arm to reduce the length (**G**). Set the arms aside keeping them covered until required. Set the leftover dark brown sugarpaste aside.

8 For the head roll 25g (⅞oz) of dark brown sugarpaste into a smooth ball and pull down the neck (**G**). Trim the neck and use this plus the sugarpaste you cut off the arms to make the facial features. Slip the head over the spaghetti at the neck and rest the head back on the cushion.

9 Roll a small ball for the nose and place in the centre of the face. Using tool no.5, mark a hole for the mouth. Add a tiny amount of pink to the dark brown sugarpaste and make two banana shapes for the lips. Using the dark brown sugarpaste, roll two small oval shapes for the eyelids and attach just above and on either side of the nose. Roll a fine lace of black sugarpaste for the eyebrows and place in a curve to outline the eyes (**G**).

10 For the headphones equally divide 2g (⅛oz) of white sugarpaste into three. Roll two cone shapes for the earpieces and lightly flatten with your finger. Equally divide

0.5g (⅛oz) of grey sugarpaste and make two much smaller cone shapes, flattening again with your finger, and place these over the top of the white. Roll the remaining white sugarpaste into a short sausage shape and place over the top of the head (**G**). Attach the earpieces to each side of the head.

11 Attach the arms to the sleeves and the hands to the earpieces. Add tiny ovals in pink sugarpaste for the fingernails. Make the bracelet by rolling 0.5g (⅛oz) of white sugarpaste into small balls and glue them around the wrist (**G**).

12 For the hair soften 25g (⅞oz) of black sugarpaste with white vegetable fat (shortening) and fill the cup of the sugar press (or garlic press). Take off some short strands and layer the back of the hair, working from the neck upwards. Make the bunches at the side by taking of a section of the hair and placing it at either side of the head. Dress the front of the hair last by arranging several strands of hair into soft folds (**G**).

The girl on the stool

1 To make the legs and the lower body roll 105g (3¾oz) of blue sugarpaste into a ball and then into a cone shape. Turn the cone so that the widest end is at the base, flatten slightly to reduce the thickness and then make a division for the legs. Soften the edges with your fingers until they are smooth, lengthening the leg at the same time, and then widen the trousers at the bottom by inserting the pointed end of tool no.3. Make a straight cut at the top of the shape for the waistline (**H**). Bend each leg at the knee area.

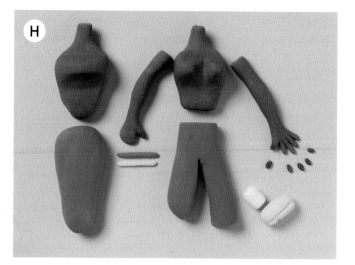

Tip
Paint the nails with confectioners' glaze to make them shine.

2 Make the shoes using 10g (⅜oz) of lime sugarpaste set aside earlier. Equally divide the sugarpaste and roll into two oval shapes. Using tool no.4, mark around the base of each shape to form the soles. Make two socks using 3g (⅛oz) of white sugarpaste equally divided. Roll into two short sausage shapes and place on top of each shoe (**H**). Push a piece of dry spaghetti down through each sock and shoe, leaving 1cm (⅜in) showing. Apply some edible glue inside the trouser bottoms and insert the shoes and socks.

3 Place the body into a sitting position on top of the stool and push a piece of dry spaghetti down through the centre and into the stool to secure. Leave 4cm (1½in) showing at the top. Position the feet apart.

4 To complete the rest of the body, head and arms you will need 47g (1⅝oz) of dark brown sugarpaste mixed together with the same quantity of light brown sugarpaste to make 94g (3⅜oz) of a lighter skin tone. Take off 54g (2oz) to shape the upper body and neck. Begin by rolling a cone shape then turn the cone around so that the widest end is at the top. Pinch out the neck then draw the paste up to form a ridge across the breasts. Indent the centre of the ridge and begin to round the shapes. Make a straight cut at the waist (**H**). Push a long piece of dry spaghetti down through the neck and into the trousers.

5 For the arms and hands equally divide 14g (½oz) of the lighter brown sugarpaste and roll out into two sausage shapes. Narrow at the wrists and elbows and flatten the palms slightly, marking out the thumbs and fingers, as described on page 16. Bend the arms at the elbows and attach ten small ovals for the fingernails made from 0.5g (⅛oz) of red sugarpaste. Set the completed arms and hands aside, keeping them covered until required.

6 For the head take 1g (⅛oz) from the remaining 26g (1oz) of the lighter brown sugarpaste and set aside for the facial features. Roll the remainder into an oval shape. Add a small ball of brown for the nose in the centre of the face. Using tool no.11, add a smile and straighten out the top lip with the soft end of your paintbrush (**I**).

7 Roll a tiny banana shape in white sugarpaste for the teeth and position them on the straight edge of the top lip. Make two banana shapes for the lips and arrange around the teeth. Roll two small cone shapes for the eyelids and secure just above and on either side of the nose. Roll two small cone shapes for the ears and attach to the side of the head, indenting the bottom with the end of your paintbrush. Roll a thin lace of black sugarpaste and underline the eyes, then make the eyebrows by rolling a small banana shape in black (**I**). Slip the head over the spaghetti at the neck.

8 For the hair soften 10g (⅜oz) of black sugarpaste with white vegetable fat (shortening) and fill the cup of the sugar press (or garlic press). Take off individual strands of hair and arrange them over the top of the head. Begin at the front and sides, taking them to the back of the head. Take off several strands of hair and twist them together to form a curl at the back, which will cover the join of the hair. To make the topknot, fill the cup of the press again and extrude longer strands. Take a larger section and curl it over to make a roll then attach this to the top of the head (**I**).

9 To make the necklace and earrings you will need 2g (⅛oz) of white sugarpaste. For the earrings, roll out the paste and cut out two 1cm (⅜in) circles, flatten them slightly then take out the centres using a 1cm (⅜in) round cutter to make loops. Attach the loops to the earlobes. Roll the remainder of the white sugarpaste into a very thin lace to make the necklace. Arrange the lace around the neckline and cross over the ends. Finish with a small ball of white where it crosses over (**I**).

10 For the top roll out 20g (¾oz) of orange sugarpaste and cut out two rectangles measuring 6 x 5cm (2⅜ x 2in). Place one piece on the back of the figure, making sure the side seams are running straight at each side. Using a 3cm (1¼in) round cutter, take out the neckline on the front of the top. Attach to the front of the figure, smoothing it around the bust area. Join the side seams neatly. Using tool no.4, mark horizontal lines across the bust area (**I**).

11 Make the sleeves using 10g (⅜oz) of orange sugarpaste equally divided. Roll into two small cone shapes, push a short piece of dry spaghetti into the shoulder area and slip the sleeves over the top.

The towel and scissors

1 For the towel roll out 10g (⅜oz) of white sugarpaste and cut out a rectangle measuring 8 x 5cm (3⅛ x 2in). Take 1g (⅛oz) of red sugarpaste and cut out two thin strips to edge the towel at either end (**J**). Place the towel over the knee of the girl on the stool. Add a few thin laces of black for the hair trimmings.

2 For the scissors roll 0.5g (⅛oz) of grey sugarpaste into a tapered cone shape and push the pointed end of tool no.3 into the fattest end to form the handle. Glue them into a crossed position and attach to the top of the towel (**J**).

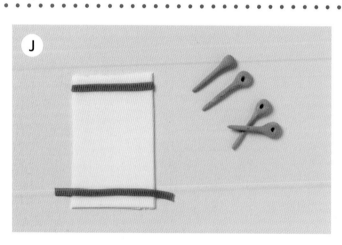

Finishing the girl on the stool

1 Position the girl on the stool behind the chair with her back nice and straight. Take the two arms you made earlier and push a short piece of dry spaghetti into the top of each arm. Attach the left bent arm to the sleeve and rest it on the back of the chair. Secure the right arm to the sleeve and place the back of the hand onto the shoulder of the girl in front for support. Drape a few strands of hair over the hands.

2 Apply some Rainbow Dust sky blue edible glitter to her eyelids to complete. To highlight the hair, lips, nails and boots, apply some confectioners' glaze.

 Girls' Night In

A Little More Fun!

Girls' World

These cute cupcake cases feature the perfect motifs for a girly gathering and co-ordinate beautifully with the main cake. The cupcakes were made using the recipe on page 22 and have been covered in pink sugarpaste, decorated with Rainbow Dust sparkle stars and topped with a flower and candle decoration all made from sugarpaste – perfect for any impromptu ladies' night!

Golfing Dreams

Have you ever had the feeling that your man loves golf more than he loves you? If so, this is the cake for him and it should score you some much-needed points too! Every little detail in this humorous cake reflects the golfing theme, and the comical scene is guaranteed to get the party guests giggling.

"Is this all the thanks I get for the gift of a treasured golf bag? Typical!"

You will need

Sugarpaste

★ 2kg 225g (4lb 14½oz) white
★ 600g (1lb 5oz) pale blue
★ 238g (8½oz) flesh
★ 144g (5⅛oz) light brown
★ 73g (2½oz) dark blue
★ 50g (1¾oz) dark brown
★ 50g (1¾oz) red
★ 48g (1⅝oz) black
★ 44g (1½oz) dark green
★ 44g (1½oz) yellow

Materials

★ 20 x 18 x 7.5cm (8 x 7 x 3in) rectangular cake
★ Dust food colour in light brown and pale pink
★ Black liquid food colour
★ Rainbow Dust starlight sparkle dust
★ White vegetable fat (shortening)
★ Pastillage (see recipe, page 23)
★ Edible glue (see page 24)

Equipment

★ 35cm (14in) square cake drum
★ 4cm (1½in), 2.5cm (1in) and 2cm (¾in) round cutters
★ 2 pimpled impression mats (optional)
★ 6 flower stamens
★ Ruler
★ Cream ribbon 15mm (½in) wide x 160cm (63in) long
★ Non-toxic glue
★ Sugar press (or garlic press)
★ Flower former
★ Basic tool kit (see pages 10–12)

Covering the cake and board . . . .

1 To cover the board you will need 700g (1lb 8⅝oz) of white sugarpaste mixed together with 100g (3½oz) of light brown sugarpaste to make a cream shade. Roll out the paste to an even 3mm (⅛in) thickness. Cover the board in the usual way (see page 28) trimming the edges neatly with a marzipan knife. Set aside to dry.

2 To cover the cake roll out 700g (1lb 8⅝oz) of white sugarpaste to an even 5mm (⅛in) thickness. Tuck in each corner of the cake neatly then continue with the sides. Trim around the edges of the cake.

The headboard and footboard . . . .

1 Transfer the templates opposite onto card. Make up some pastillage (see recipe, page 23) coloured with light brown dust food colour. Take off 250g (8¾oz) of pastillage and roll out to an even 5mm (⅛in) thickness.

2 For the headboard place the large template on top of the pastillage and cut around it using a cutting wheel (or pizza cutter). Mark the centre using a straight pin and position the shaped edge of the card 1.5cm (½in) below the top line on the pastillage piece. Using a ruler, mark vertical lines from the centre outwards, taking the lines down to the bottom of the piece (**A**). Set aside on a flat non-stick surface, turning over after 12 hours.

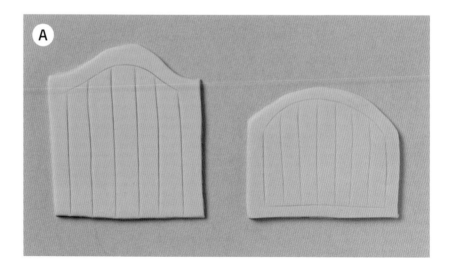

Tip

Pastillage dries very quickly, so it is essential that any unused paste is covered to prevent air getting to it.

3 To make the footboard roll out the remaining pastillage to an even 5mm (⅛in) thickness and cut around the smaller template. Place the card 1cm (⅜in) from the top of the pastillage piece and mark around it. Using a ruler, mark lines vertically down the centre but stop the line 1cm (⅜in) from the bottom of the piece. When the lines are complete, mark a horizontal line across the bottom (**A**).

4 When both pieces are dry, attach to the top and bottom of the cake using strong edible glue. Make this by mixing some pastillage and edible glue together into a stiff paste. Set aside to dry. When you come to serve the cake, remove the headboard and footboard before cutting.

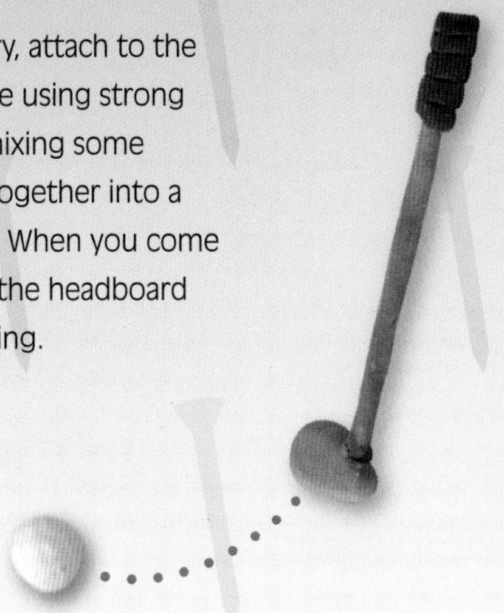

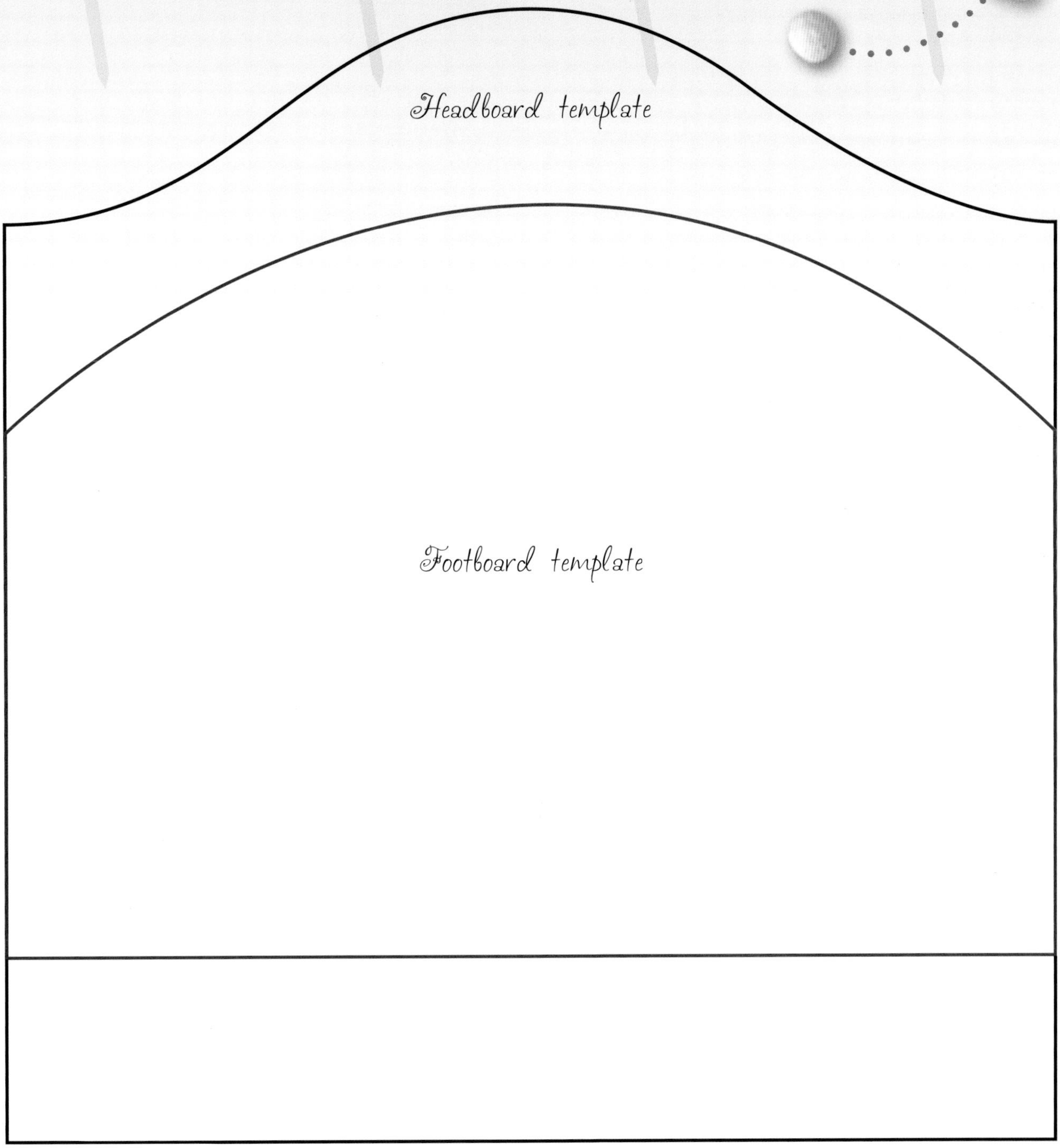

Headboard template

Footboard template

The bedside tables

1 For the drawers take 80g (2⅞oz) of white sugarpaste and roll into a fat sausage shape then continue to smooth and shape it into a rectangular prism measuring 6cm (2⅜in) high x 4cm (1½in) wide x 3cm (1¼in) deep (**B**). Place the shape flat onto a non-stick work surface or a dusted board.

2 Make two draw fronts by rolling out 6g (¼oz) of white sugarpaste. Cut into two rectangles measuring 2 x 3cm (¾ x 1¼in) and attach to the front of the draws. Mark a border inside each shape using tool no.4 (**B**).

3 Make the draw knobs by rolling 1g (⅛oz) of white sugarpaste into two balls. Using the point of tool no.5, mark both knobs to look like golf balls and then attach to the centre of each draw front (**B**).

4 For the feet roll 4g (⅛oz) of white sugarpaste into four balls and set aside until they harden off. Push four short pieces of dry spaghetti into each corner at the base of the draws and attach the feet. Stand the draws upright.

5 Make the top by rolling out 7g (¼oz) of white sugarpaste cut out a rectangle measuring 4 x 3cm (1½ x 1¼in) and place on the top (**B**). Make a second bedside table in exactly the same way.

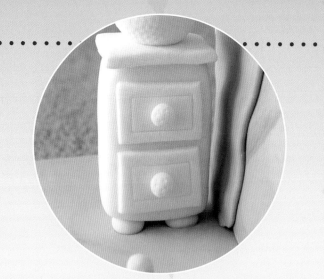

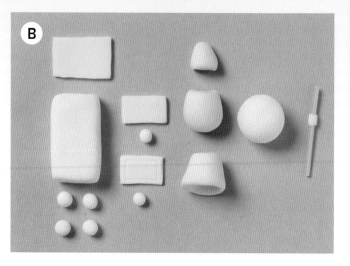

B

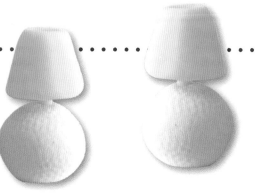

The lamps

1 For the base roll 21g (¾oz) of white sugarpaste into a ball. Place the ball in between two pimpled impression mats and roll until textured. Place the lamp base on top of the bedside table and push a piece of dry spaghetti down through the centre of the lamp and into the top of the draws, leaving 3cm (¼in) showing at the top. Roll a tiny ball of white sugarpaste and push it down the spaghetti to rest on top of the lamp base (**B**).

2 To make the shade roll 18g (¾oz) of yellow sugarpaste into a cone shape and cut off one-third from the narrow end. Using tool no.3, hollow out the shape and smooth the edges with your fingers (**B**). Attach the shade to the top of the spaghetti. Make two. Set the bedside tables and lamps aside until you have completed the bedspread.

Tip

If you do not have the textured mats, you can mark the pimples by hand using the end of a piece of dry spaghetti.

The pillows

1 For two pillows equally divide 170g (6oz) of white sugarpaste and roll into two sausage shapes 8cm (3⅛in) long. Roll over the top of each sausage to make a piece 7cm (2¾in) high x 9cm (3½in) wide x 1.5cm (½in) deep (**C**). Place one pillow on the right-hand side of the bed for the man's pillow, which has no frill.

2 Make a third pillow using 72g (2½oz) of white sugarpaste rolled into a sausage shape 8cm (3⅛in) long. Complete as before, but making this pillow 6cm (2⅜in) high.

3 To make frills for two pillows roll 50g (1¾oz) of white sugarpaste into a strip measuring 4 x 30cm (1½ x 12in). Cut the strip in half lengthwise. Hold the end of each strip with your left hand and as you pass the length of sugarpaste from your right hand, fold it gently into a frill, but do not crack it. Once you have frilled the strip it should all be in your left hand. Place it down onto the work surface then flatten the top edge to hold the pleats. Make this edge straight and attach around the top and sides of the large and smaller pillow (**C**). Place the large pillow at the back and the smaller one in front on the left-hand side of the bed.

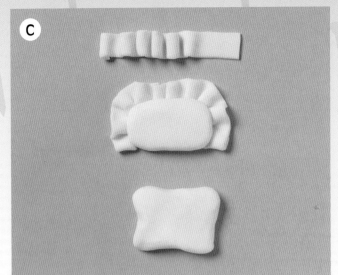

C

Tip

Do not add CMC to the paste for the frill as it will crack – it should be very supple.

The wife

1 For the body roll 74g (2½oz) of flesh-coloured sugarpaste into a cone shape and pull out the neck at the thickest end. Soften the shoulders and shape the bust area by pushing the sugarpaste from the top and bottom to form a ridge. Mark the ridge in the centre to divide the two breasts. Soften and round the shape (**D**). Set aside.

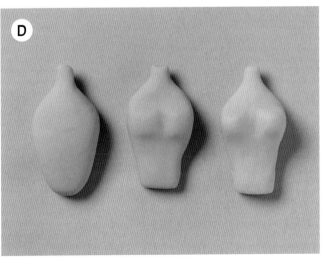

D

2 To make the basque roll out 6g (¼oz) of red sugarpaste and cut out two 2cm (¾in) circles. Attach one to each breast. Make the remainder of the bodice by rolling out 20g (¾oz) of red sugarpaste into a rectangle measuring 6 x 13cm (2⅜ x 5in). Place the piece centrally over the body and taking a 2cm (¾in) circle, mark the underside of the cups. Remove the piece and cut out the shapes (**E**). Apply some edible glue around body, secure in place at the front and wrap around the back making a neat join. Place the body in front of the pillows and push a piece of dry spaghetti down through the centre and into the cake. Push a short piece of dry spaghetti into the shoulder area.

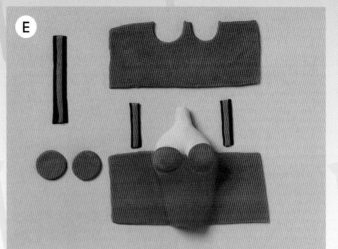

3 For the straps roll out 1g (⅛oz) of black sugarpaste. Using tool no.4, cut out a strip measuring 10cm x 4mm (4 x ⅛in). Then roll out 0.5g (⅛oz) of red sugarpaste and cut out a thinner strip, the same length but half the width of the black. Place the red strip down the centre of the black strip then cut in half to make two straps and set aside (**E**).

4 To make the arms roll 30g (1oz) of flesh-coloured sugarpaste into a sausage shape. Make a diagonal cut in the centre and press lightly at the rounded ends to form the hands. Narrow each arm at the wrist and elbow. Mark the thumbs and soften the edges. Mark the remainder of each hand into four fingers. Separate each one and roll into a smooth shape. Bend each arm at the elbow and arrange in a folded position (**F**).

5 Make the fingernails using 0.5g (⅛oz) of red sugarpaste, rolling ten tiny oval shapes. Attach to each finger with edible glue. To make the ring, roll 0.5g (⅛oz) of yellow sugarpaste into a thin lace and cut off a short piece to fit around the third finger on the left hand. Attach the folded arms over the spaghetti at the shoulders, securing them firmly. Support them underneath with some foam if necessary to keep them in place until dry. When dry, attach the basque straps over each shoulder to hide the join.

6 For the legs equally divide 60g (2oz) of flesh-coloured sugarpaste. Roll into two sausage shapes and turn up one end of each to form the feet. Bend the right leg at the knee and attach to the front of the body. Make the left leg to lie outstretched (**F**).

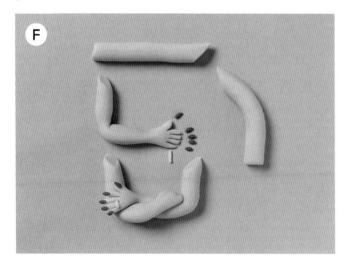

7 For the head roll 30g (1oz) of flesh-coloured sugarpaste into a ball and indent the eye area (see page 14). Using 1g (⅛oz) of flesh-coloured sugarpaste, roll a tiny ball for the nose and secure to the centre of the face. From 1g (⅛oz) of white sugarpaste, take off two small balls for the eyes. Place just above and on either side of the nose. Make two smaller balls in dark brown sugarpaste and attach over the whites, these should be looking directly to the left. Finally add an even smaller ball of black to each eye (**G**).

8 For the ears make two small cone shapes and attach to the side of the head, keeping the top of the ear running in line with the centre of the eye. Indent the bottom of each ear with the end of your paintbrush (**G**).

9 To make the lips roll two small banana shapes in red sugarpaste. Place the top lip into position and the bottom lip slightly to the right and not in line (**G**).

10 For the eyelashes take 1g (⅛oz) of black sugarpaste and roll into a very thin strip measuring 1 x 2cm (⅜ x ¾in). Using tool no.4, make cuts along the base of the strip. Cut the strip in half, then curve the lashes upwards over the end of your paintbrush. Secure over the top of each eye with edible glue.

11 Apply some edible glue to the neck area and slip the head over the spaghetti. Turn the head towards where the husband will be. Dust the cheeks with pale pink dust food colour.

12 For the hair soften 40g (1½oz) of black sugarpaste with white vegetable fat (shortening). Take off enough sugarpaste to fill the cup of the sugar press (or garlic press), extruding short strands of hair to go around the back and sides of the head. Begin by placing the hair on the hairline at the back of the head then take it up to the crown, working around to each side (**G**).

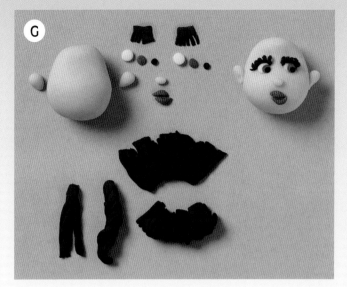

13 Keep refilling the sugar press and dress the front of the head, turning the hair up and over to make a roll. Make the ringlet to the side of the head by extruding longer strands and twisting them together (**G**). Attach to the side of the head, resting the end on the body.

The husband

1 To complete the husband you will need 232g (8¼oz) of beige sugarpaste – make this by mixing together 190g (6¾oz) of white sugarpaste with 42g (1½oz) of light brown. Roll 90g (3¼oz) into a fat cone shape to make the body. Make the pyjama collar using 12g (½oz) rolled out and cut into a 4cm (1½in) circle, then take out one-third of the circle with a 2.5cm (1in) round cutter (**H**). Soften the edges of the collar and place around the top of the body. Place the body on top of the bed, just resting on the edge of the pillow and push a short piece of dry spaghetti into the shoulder.

2 For the legs equally divide 100g (3½oz) of beige sugarpaste and roll into two sausage shapes. Turn up the feet at the ends. Attach to the body, crossing one leg over the other in a sleeping position (**H**).

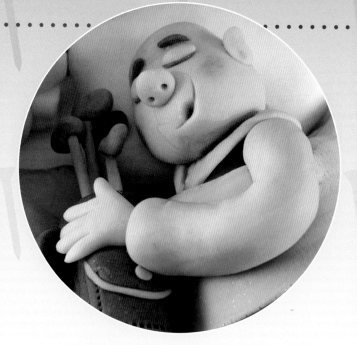

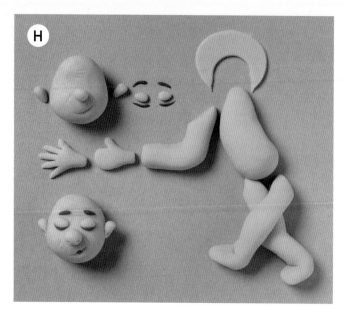

Tip

Just make simple shapes for the legs and feet, as they will be hidden under the bedspread.

3 For the arm roll 30g (1oz) of beige sugarpaste into a sausage shape. Bend the arm at the elbow and make a diagonal cut at the top. Attach the arm to the shoulder and push a short piece of dry spaghetti into the wrist. Make the hand using 4g (⅛oz) of flesh-coloured sugarpaste rolled into a cone shape and make the fingers as described on page 16 (**H**). Make a straight cut at the wrist and slip over the spaghetti.

4 For the head you will need 38g (1⅜oz) of flesh-coloured sugarpaste. Take off 1g (⅛oz) and set aside for the nose, ears and eyelids, then roll the remainder into a ball. Indent the eye area (see page 14) and then place the head inside a flower former (**H**).

5 Push a short piece of dry spaghetti into the centre of the face and roll a cone shape for the nose. Slip the nose over the spaghetti and mark two nostrils with tool no.5. Make two small oval shapes for the eyelids and place just above and on either side of the nose. Mark the mouth to one side using tool no.11, then insert the end of your paintbrush to open it up a little. Using 0.5g (⅛oz) of dark brown sugarpaste, roll a very thin lace and place under each eyelid then add eyebrows by rolling two small banana shapes (**H**). Dust the cheeks with pale pink dust food colour.

The bedspread

To make the bedspread you will need 600g (1lb 5oz) of pale blue sugarpaste and 50g (1¾oz) of dark blue. Randomly mix together the two colours to make it look shaded, then roll out to a measurement of 36 x 22cm (14 x 8½in). Turn over 4cm (1½in) at the top and 1cm (⅜in) at the bottom and arrange over the bed. Once you have the bedspread in place, secure it to the sides of the bed with edible glue. Put the bedside tables into place on either side of the bed. Lightly dust the bedspread with Rainbow Dust starlight sparkle dust and a dry brush.

The golf bag

1 For the bag roll 35g (1¼oz) of dark brown sugarpaste into a sausage shape 6cm (2⅜in) long. Flatten the ends and, using tool no.4, mark a ridge around the top and bottom. Roll 2g (⅛oz) of light brown sugarpaste into a very thin lace and apply over the marks at the top and bottom of the bag (**I**). Set the remaining light brown sugarpaste aside for use later.

2 For the front pocket roll out 2g (⅛oz) of dark brown sugarpaste into a rectangle measuring 3 x 2cm (1¼ x ¾in). Round off the top with tool no.4 then fold the rounded edge over. Using tool no.12, stitch mark around the side and bottom of the pocket. Attach to the front of the bag. Using the leftover light brown sugarpaste, decorate the pocket by adding a small round ball on the flap then roll a thin lace in the same colour to edge the curve of the pocket. Make four small balls for the studs at the base of the bag (**I**).

3 To make the strap roll out 2g (⅛oz) of dark brown sugarpaste into a thin sausage shape. Lightly press on the top with your rolling pin to flatten and cut to a length of 8cm (3⅛in). Attach to the side of the bag (**I**).

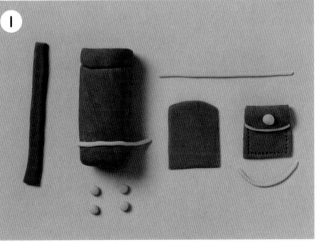

Tip
Indent holes at the top of the bag to enable the clubs to be inserted easily.

The golf clubs

1 To complete all the golf clubs make 14g (½oz) of grey sugarpaste by mixing together 13g (½oz) of white and 1g (⅛oz) of black. To make the clubs for the bag, thinly roll out the grey sugarpaste and cut six strips measuring 1 x 3.5cm (⅜ x 1⅜in). Apply some edible glue down each strip and place a longer length of dry spaghetti on the top. Fold over the strip to cover the spaghetti then remove any surplus sugarpaste with tool no.4. Roll the piece on the work surface to reduce the bulk then trim one end leaving 5mm (⅛in) of spaghetti showing at the bottom and 1cm (⅜in) at the top to push into the bag (**J**).

2 Make three grey club heads by rolling 1.5g (⅛oz) of grey sugarpaste into three small cone shapes (**J**). Flatten a little with your fingers and slip the heads over the spaghetti at the base of each shaft.

3 Make one black club head as before, using 0.5g (⅛oz) of black sugarpaste and push on to the shaft (**J**). Allow the clubs to dry and then push them into the holes at the top of the bag. Place the completed bag on the bed, with the husband's hand on the top.

4 Make two more clubs with longer shafts to go on the board. Roll out the grey sugarpaste and cut two strips measuring 6 x 3.5cm (2⅜ x 1⅜in). Make the shafts as before but leaving only 0.5cm (⅛in) of spaghetti showing at the base. Make the grips by rolling out 1g (⅛oz) of brown

sugarpaste and cutting two pieces measuring 2 x 1.5cm (¾ x ½in) (**J**). Apply some edible glue around the top of each shaft and roll the piece around, trimming off any surplus. Using tool no.4, mark horizontal lines around to finish. Make two more club heads using the grey sugarpaste and slip over the spaghetti (**J**). Attach one club to the base of the bed and the other to the front of the cake board.

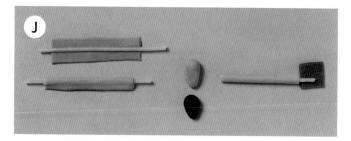

The cat

1 To complete the cat you will need 50g (1¾oz) of grey sugarpaste, made by mixing together 45g (1½oz) of white sugarpaste with 5g (¼oz) of black. Take off 20g (¾oz) and roll into a cone shape for the body (**K**).

2 For the back legs equally divide 10g (⅜oz) and roll into two cone shapes then narrow the legs, leaving the paws nicely rounded. Attach to the body and mark the paws using tool no.4 (**K**).

3 For the front legs roll 5g (¼oz) into a sausage shape and make a diagonal cut in the centre. Attach to the body and mark the paws as before (**K**). Push a short piece of dry spaghetti into the neck to support the head.

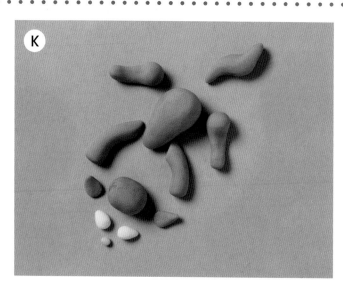

4 For the head roll 8g (¼oz) into a ball and slip over the spaghetti at the neck. For the cheeks, equally divide 1g (⅛oz) of white sugarpaste and make two small cone shapes. Attach in the centre of the face with the rounded ends of the cones together. Roll a tiny ball of flesh-coloured sugarpaste for the nose and place on top of the cheeks. Using tool no.11, mark the eyes as though asleep (**K**).

5 For the ears equally divide 1g (⅛oz) of grey sugarpaste, make two cone shapes and attach to the sides of the head using tool no.1. Roll 6g (¼oz) of the grey sugarpaste into a fat cone shape for the tail, make a diagonal cut at the thickest end and attach to the back of the cat (**K**).

6 For the whiskers take six flower stamens and cut off the rounded tips. Push three into each cheek. Attach the cat on top of the bed, resting on the wife's legs.

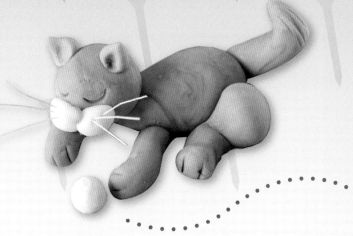

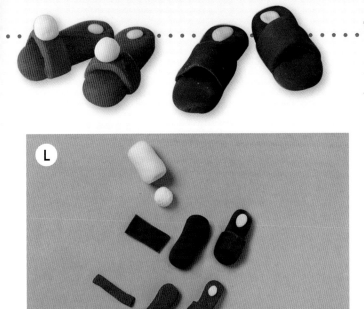

The slippers

1 For her slippers roll 6g (¼oz) of red sugarpaste into a sausage shape for the sole, and then press lightly with your finger to flatten. Roll a strap to go over the top using 1g (⅛oz) of red sugarpaste. Roll 0.5g (⅛oz) of white sugarpaste into a tiny flattened teardrop shape for the label at the back of the slipper and roll a further 0.5g (⅛oz) of white sugarpaste into a small golf ball for the front (**L**). Make two and attach to her side of the bed.

2 For his slippers roll 6g (¼oz) of dark green sugarpaste into a sausage shape and press with your finger to flatten. Roll out 1g (⅛oz) of dark green sugarpaste and cut a strip to go across the top of the slipper. Make a small teardrop shape with 0.5g (⅛oz) of white sugarpaste to make a label and then flatten and attach to the slipper (**L**). Make two and place them centrally on his side of the bed.

The loose golf balls and the holder

1 Make ten golf balls by dividing 4g (⅛oz) of white sugarpaste into ten and texture as before (**L**). Place one beside the cat on the bed and arrange the others around the board.

2 For the holder roll 7g (¼oz) of yellow sugarpaste into a short sausage shape. Flatten one end and insert the pointed end of tool no.3 inside the other end to hollow it out. Attach to the front of the board and place a golf ball at the opening (**L**).

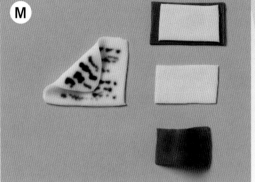

The newspaper and the book

1 Make a single sheet of newspaper by rolling out 10g (⅜oz) of white sugarpaste into a rectangle measuring 4 x 5cm (1½ x 2in). Using a fine paintbrush and some black liquid food colour, doodle some print. When dry, fold over the top left corner into the centre and add more print to the top (**M**). Attach to the board in front of his bedside table.

2 For the book cover roll out 4g (⅛oz) of dark brown sugarpaste to a measurement of 3 x 5.5cm (1¼ x 2⅛in) and keep flat. Using 6g (¼oz) of white sugarpaste, cut out two rectangles for the pages measuring 2.5 x 5cm (1 x 2in). Glue the pages to the open cover and then fold the book in half. Using tool no.4, mark the spine, being careful not to press too hard. Open the book out, turn it upside down and secure on the edge of the newspaper (**M**).

The cap, shoes, socks and towel

1 To make the cap roll 17g (½oz) of dark blue sugarpaste into a ball and press onto the work surface to flatten the base. Make the peak by rolling out 6g (¼oz) of dark blue sugarpaste and cutting out a 4cm (1½in) circle. Take out one-third of the circle with the edge of the cutter, and using tool no.4, cut a straight line down either side (**N**). Secure the peak to the crown of the hat with edible glue. Attach on the right-hand side of the board.

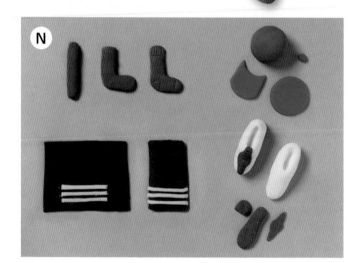

2 To make the shoes equally divide 20g (¾oz) of white sugarpaste and roll into two sausage shapes. Using tool no.1, hollow out the back end of each shoe and smooth the edges with your finger. Make the soles using 6g (¼oz) of dark brown sugarpaste equally divided, and rolled into two sausage shapes. Flatten with your finger, narrow in the centre slightly and apply edible glue on the top (**N**). Place each upper onto each sole and press lightly.

3 Make a small heel for each shoe by rolling 0.5g (⅛oz) of dark brown sugarpaste into a flattened ball. Make a straight cut, shaping it into a semi-circle, keeping the round edge outside and attach under the sole. Make the front decoration for each shoe by rolling 0.5g (⅛oz) of brown sugarpaste into a banana shape, then press out the middle to widen the shape. Taper the ends and attach down the front of each shoe, then mark the laces across with tool no.4 (**N**).

4 For the socks equally divide 10g (⅜oz) of red sugarpaste, roll into two sausage shapes and flatten. Bend into shape to look like socks. Using tool no.12, stitch mark the heels, across the toes and the tops (**N**). Attach the shoes to the cake board and drape the socks over them.

5 For the towel roll out 30g (1oz) of dark green sugarpaste and cut out a 9cm (3½in) square. Roll out 2g (⅛oz) of white sugarpaste and cut three stripes 6cm (2⅜in) long. Attach at the bottom of the towel in the centre then fold into three and hang over the end of the bed (**N**).

Golfing Dreams

A Little More Fun!

Tee Time

If you are having a large birthday party, making matching cupcakes will make the cake go much further. These fantastic golf-themed paper cases mean you can match your cupcakes to the main cake perfectly. These cakes were made using the recipe on page 22, then covered with a circle of white sugarpaste that has been impressed with a textured rolling pin and then decorated with a variety of golfing motifs.

Suppliers

UK

Jane Asher Party Cakes
24 Cale Street, London SW3 3QU
+44 (0) 20 7584 6177
info@janeasher.com
www.jane-asher.co.uk
Sugarcraft supplies

Berisfords Ribbons
PO Box 2, Thomas Street,
Congleton, Cheshire CW12 1EF
+44 (0) 1260 274011
office@berisfords-ribbons.co.uk
www.berisfords-ribbons.co.uk
Ribbons – see website for stockists

The British Sugarcraft Guild
Wellington House, Messeter Place,
London SE9 5DP
+44 (0) 20 8859 6943
nationaloffice@bsguk.org
www.bsguk.org
*Exhibitions, courses,
members' benefits*

Ceefor Cakes
PO Box 443, Leighton Buzzard,
Bedfordshire LU7 1AJ
+44 (0) 1525 375237
info@ceeforcakes.co.uk
www.ceeforcakes.co.uk
*Cake and display boxes,
sugarcraft supplies*

The Craft Company
Unit 6/7 Queens Park, Queensway,
Leamington Spa CV31 3LH
+44 (0) 1926 888507
info@craftcompany.co.uk
www.craftcompany.co.uk
*Boxes, boards, decorations,
edibles, tools and ribbons*

Maisie Parrish
Maisie's World, 840 High Lane, Chell,
Stoke on Trent, Staffordshire ST6 6HG
+44 (0) 1782 876090
maisie.parrish@ntlworld.com
www.maisieparrish.com
*Novelty cake decorating, one-to-
one tuition, workshops and demos*

Guy Paul & Co. Ltd
Unit 10 The Business Centre,
Corinium Industrial Estate,
Raans Road, Amersham,
Buckinghamshire HP6 6FB
+44 (0) 1494 432121
sales@guypaul.co.uk
www.guypaul.co.uk
Sugarcraft and bakery supplies

Pinch of Sugar
1256 Leek Road, Abbey Hulton,
Stoke on Trent ST2 8BP
+44 (0) 1782 570557
sales@pinchofsugar.co.uk
www.pinchofsugar.co.uk
*Bakeware, tools, boards and
boxes, sugarcraft supplies, ribbons,
colours, decorations and candles*

Renshaws
Crown Street, Liverpool L8 7RF
+44 (0) 870 870 6954
enquiries@renshaw-nbf.co.uk
www.renshaw-nbf.co.uk
*Caramels, Regalice sugarpastes,
marzipans and compounds*

Alan Silverwood Ltd
Ledsam House, Ledsam Street,
Birmingham B16 8DN
+44 (0) 121 454 3571
sales@alan-silverwood.co.uk
www.alansilverwood.co.uk
Bakeware, multi-mini cake pans

Squires Group
Squires House, 3 Waverley Lane,
Farnham, Surrey GU9 8BB
+44 (0) 1252 711749
info@squires-group.co.uk
www.squires-shop.com
*Bakeware, tools, boards, sugarcraft
supplies, ribbons, edible gold and
silver leaf, decorations and candles*

Rainbow Dust
Unit 3, Cuerden Green Mill,
Lostock Hall, Preston PR5 5LP
+44 (0) 1772 322335
info@rainbowdust.co.uk
www.rainbowdust.co.uk
*Dust food colours, pens and
edible cake decorations*

USA

All In One Bake Shop
8566 Research Blvd, Austin, TX 78758
+1 512 371 3401
info@allinonebakeshop.com
www.allinonebakeshop.com
*Cake making and
decorating supplies*

Beryl Cake Decorating Supplies
PO Box 1584 N. Springfield, VA 22151
+1 800 488 2749
beryls@beryls.com
www.beryls.com
*Cake decorating and
pastry supplies*

European Cake Gallery
844 North Crowley Road,
Crowley, TX 76036
+1 817 297 2240
info@thesugarart.com
www.europeancakegallery.us
www.thesugarart.com
Cake and sugarcraft supplies

Global Sugar Art
7 Plattsburgh Plaza,
Plattsburgh, NY 12901
+1 800 420 6088
info@globalsugarart.com
www.globalsugarart.com
Everything sugarcraft

**Wilton School of Cake
Decorating and Confectionery Art**
7511 Lemont Road, Darien, IL 60561
+1 630 985 6077
wiltonschool@wilton.com
www.wilton.com
*Bakeware and cake decorating
supplies, tuition*

BRAZIL

Boloarte
Rue Enes De Souza, 35 – Tijuca,
Rio De Janeiro RJ – CEP 20521 – 210
+55 (21) 2571 2242/2317 9231
cursos@boloarte.com.br
www.boloarte.com.br
*Cake decorating, sugarcraft
supplies and events*

NETHERLANDS

Planet Cake
Zuidplein 117, 3083 CN,
Rotterdam
+31 (0) 10 290 9130
info@cake.nl www.cake.nl
Cake making/decorating supplies

AUSTRALIA

Planet Cake
106 Beattie Street,
Balmain, NSW 2041
+61 (2) 9810 3843
info@planetcake.com.au
www.planetcake.com.au
*Cake making and
decorating supplies*

About the Author

*Maisie Parrish is often told she has magic hands, and when she begins
to work something magical does indeed happen …*

Maisie is completely self-taught and her cute and colourful characters have a
unique quality that is instantly recognizable and much copied. Over the last few
years, she has been very busy travelling to many different countries, teaching
and demonstrating her skills. She was honoured to be the prime demonstrator
for the New Zealand Cake Guild, and became an honourary member of the
Victoria Cake Guild in Australia. She is a tutor at The Wilton School of Cake
Decorating in Chicago, The International School of Culinary Education in New
York, Caljava International School of Cake Decorating in California and Squires
Kitchen International School of Sugarcraft in England to mention a few. She
is also an accredited demonstrator for the British Sugarcraft Guild.

Her fans travel thousands of miles to visit her home studio in
Stoke on Trent, England, for a chance to be taught by the master.
People find it difficult to believe that she never actually bakes cakes
for anyone, she considers herself to be a sugar artist who can visit
as many as three countries in a month.

Maisie has enjoyed several television appearances, including *The Good
Food Show* and *QVC*, and she is the author of nine books, with more titles
in the pipeline. Further examples of her work can be seen on her website,
www.maisieparrish.com where she welcomes you into **Maisie's World**.

Acknowledgments

My grateful thanks to Renshaws for generously supplying me with their wonderful range of readymade sugarpaste. The beautiful colours in their range have helped me to create so many lovely characters and make this book outstanding. The photography by Simon Whitmore brings to life the magical quality of each project, so beautifully staged by Victoria Marks. So much encouragement and help has been given to me in the making of this book by the editorial staff of David & Charles, particularly by Jennifer Fox-Proverbs and Jeni Hennah, with my special thanks to Ame Verso for her brilliant editorial touch.

Index